*f*RESH *f*OODS

Publications International, Ltd.
Favorite Brand Name Recipes at www.fbnr.com

Microwave Cooking: Microwave ovens vary in wattage. Use the cooking times as guidelines and check for doneness before adding more time.

Preparation/Cooking Times: Preparation times are based on the approximate amount of time required to assemble the recipe before cooking, baking, chilling or serving. These times include preparation steps such as measuring, chopping and mixing. The fact that some preparations and cooking can be done simultaneously is taken into account. Preparation of optional ingredients and serving suggestions is not included.

Table of contents

Fresh foods, *Fresh* flavors

Celebrate the bounty of fresh foods—from fruits straight from orchards and citrus groves to vegetables fresh from the farm. Team them with fresh meats, poultry, seafood, eggs and herbs to add zest to your menus. Increasing the fresh produce in your diet rewards you with bold flavors and crisp textures—plus seasonal fruits and vegetables are a healthy addition to anyone's diet. Even a few meals a week with fresh ingredients, especially fruits and vegetables, will increase your intake of important vitamins, minerals and fiber. Cooking with fresh ingredients doesn't need to take much time; this cookbook offers many quick-to-fix recipes, some featuring convenience products, that are a snap to make. Teriyaki Salmon with Asian Slaw (page 38), which includes packaged coleslaw mix and purchased teriyaki sauce, can be ready in less than 25 minutes. The recipe for Guacamole (page 10) can be prepared in less time than it takes to thaw a frozen guacamole dip—and the flavor is so much better.

Fresh Foods features over 150 recipes for appetizers, entrées, side dishes, soups and stews, salads, desserts and brunch recipes. This wonderful cookbook is filled with lots of photographs that will inspire you to prepare these colorful foods. Enjoy hearty main dishes, such as stir-fries, stews and sandwiches, and find new ideas for side dishes, like Savory Skillet Broccoli (page 110) or Cheese Stuffed Pattypans (page 118). Start a weekend morning with a special breakfast or brunch of a healthy version of Eggs Benedict (page 206) or a delicious Cranberry Streusel Coffee Cake (page 194). Sweet treats have not been forgotten. Try Speedy Pineapple-Lime Sorbet (page 154) on a hot summer day or Hot Rum-Glazed Bananas over Ice Cream (page 156) to complete a special dinner. What tasty ways to add more fruit to your diet!

*D*on't waste another minute—add healthy foods, bold flavors and lively colors to your family's meals by cooking and baking with fresh foods.

Great
beginnings

Vegetable-Topped Hummus

1 can (about 15 ounces) chick-peas, rinsed and drained
2 tablespoons tahini
2 tablespoons lemon juice
1 clove garlic
¾ teaspoon salt
1 medium tomato, finely chopped
2 green onions, finely chopped
2 tablespoons chopped fresh parsley

1. Combine chick-peas, tahini, lemon juice, garlic and salt in food processor or blender; process until smooth.

2. Combine tomato, onions and parsley in small bowl.

3. Place chick-pea mixture in medium serving bowl; spoon tomato mixture evenly over top. Serve with wedges of pita bread or assorted crackers.

Makes 8 servings

Spinach-Cheese Bundles

1 container (6½ ounces) garlic-and-herb-flavored spreadable cheese
½ cup chopped fresh spinach
¼ teaspoon black pepper
1 package (17¼ ounces) frozen puff pastry, thawed
Sweet and sour sauce or favorite dipping sauce (optional)

1. Preheat oven to 400°F. Combine spreadable cheese, spinach and pepper in small bowl; mix well.

2. Roll out one sheet puff pastry dough on floured surface into 12-inch square. Cut into 16 (3-inch) squares. Place about 1 teaspoon cheese mixture in center of each square. Brush edges of square with water. Bring edges up and together over filling and twist tightly to seal; fan out corners of puff pastry. Repeat with remaining sheets of puff pastry and cheese mixture.

3. Place bundles 2 inches apart on ungreased baking sheet. Bake about 13 minutes or until golden brown. Serve warm with dipping sauce, if desired. *Makes 32 bundles*

Pineapple-Ginger Shrimp Cocktail

9 fresh pineapple spears (about 1 package), divided
¼ cup all-fruit apricot preserves
1 tablespoon finely chopped onion
½ teaspoon grated fresh ginger
⅛ teaspoon black pepper
8 ounces cooked medium shrimp (about 30)
1 red or green bell pepper, cored and cut into 12 strips

1. Chop 3 pineapple spears into bite-size pieces; combine with preserves, onion, ginger and black pepper in medium bowl.

2. Arrange shrimp, bell pepper strips and remaining pineapple spears in 6 cocktail glasses. Spoon pineapple mixture over top. *Makes 6 servings*

Guacamole

- 2 large avocados, peeled and pitted
- ¼ cup finely chopped tomato
- 2 tablespoons grated onion with juice
- 2 tablespoons lime juice or lemon juice
- ½ teaspoon salt
- ¼ teaspoon hot pepper sauce
- Black pepper

Place avocados in medium bowl; mash coarsely with fork. Stir in tomato, onion, lime juice, salt and pepper sauce; mix well. Add black pepper to taste. Spoon into serving container. Serve immediately, or cover and refrigerate up to 2 hours. Garnish with additional chopped tomatoes, if desired.

Makes 2 cups

Summer Fruits with Peanut Butter-Honey Dip

- ⅓ cup smooth or chunky peanut butter
- 2 tablespoons milk
- 2 tablespoons honey
- 1 tablespoon apple juice or water
- ⅛ teaspoon ground cinnamon
- 2 cups melon balls, including cantaloupe and honeydew
- 1 peach or nectarine, pitted and cut into 8 wedges
- 1 banana, peeled and thickly sliced

1. Place peanut butter in small bowl; gradually stir in milk and honey until blended. Stir in apple juice and cinnamon until mixture is smooth.

2. Serve dip with prepared fruits for dipping.

Makes 4 servings (about ½ cup dip)

Serving Suggestion: This dip is the perfect end to a spicy Thai or Oriental dinner.

Creamy Salsa Dip

1 ½ cups prepared **HIDDEN VALLEY®** The Original Ranch® Dressing
2 tomatoes, peeled, seeded and chopped
½ cup shredded Monterey Jack cheese
¼ cup sliced almonds
¼ cup mild or hot green chile peppers, seeded and minced
1 green onion, finely chopped
   Additional sliced almonds
   Fresh cilantro

In medium bowl, combine all ingredients except additional almonds and cilantro; mix well. Refrigerate at least 1 hour before serving. Garnish with additional almonds and cilantro. Serve with taco chips or fresh vegetables.

Makes about 2 cups

Alouette® Garlic and Herb Croustade

1 tablespoon olive oil
1 cup chopped baby portobello or other mushroom
⅔ cup chopped roasted red bell pepper
½ cup minced onion
½ cup chopped blanched bacon
1 teaspoon chopped garlic
1 (6.5-ounce) or 2 (4-ounce) packages **ALOUETTE®** Garlic et Herbes
2 tablespoons fresh parsley (or 1 tablespoon dried)
2 (2-ounce) packages mini phyllo shells

In a nonstick pan over medium heat, heat oil and sauté baby portobello, red bell pepper, onion, bacon and garlic for 3 to 5 minutes. Reduce heat to low and add Alouette. Blend and simmer for a minute. Remove from heat and stir in parsley. Spoon a heaping teaspoonful into each phyllo cup and serve warm.

Makes 30 appetizers

Tip: For a creative touch, use any variety of seasonally fresh vegetables, such as chopped fennel or summer or winter squash.

Mini Vegetable Quiches

2 cups cut-up vegetables (bell peppers, broccoli, zucchini and/or carrots)
2 tablespoons chopped green onion
2 tablespoons FLEISCHMANN'S® Original Margarine
4 (8-inch) flour tortillas, each cut into 8 triangles
1 cup EGG BEATERS® Healthy Real Egg Product
1 cup fat-free (skim) milk
½ teaspoon dried basil leaves

In medium nonstick skillet, over medium-high heat, sauté vegetables and green onion in margarine until tender.

Arrange 4 tortilla pieces in each of 8 (6-ounce) greased custard cups or ramekins, placing points of tortilla pieces at center of bottom of each cup and pressing lightly to form shape of cup. Divide vegetable mixture evenly among cups. In small bowl, combine Egg Beaters®, milk and basil. Pour evenly over vegetable mixture. Place cups on baking sheet. Bake at 375°F for 20 to 25 minutes or until puffed and knife inserted into centers comes out clean. Let stand 5 minutes before serving.   *Makes 8 servings*

BelGioioso® Fontina Melt

1 loaf Italian or French bread
2 fresh tomatoes, cubed
   Basil leaves, julienned
   BELGIOIOSO® Fontina Cheese, sliced

Cut bread lengthwise into halves. Top each half with tomatoes and sprinkle with basil. Top with BelGioioso Fontina Cheese. Place in oven at 350°F for 10 to 12 minutes or until cheese is golden brown.
Makes 6 to 8 servings

Thai-Style Pork Kabobs

⅓ cup reduced-sodium soy sauce
2 tablespoons fresh lime juice
2 tablespoons water
2 teaspoons hot chili oil*
2 cloves garlic, minced
1 teaspoon minced fresh ginger
12 ounces well-trimmed pork tenderloin
1 red or yellow bell pepper, cut into ½-inch chunks
1 red or sweet onion, cut into ½-inch chunks
2 cups hot cooked rice (optional)

*If hot chili oil is not available, combine 2 teaspoons vegetable oil and ½ teaspoon red pepper flakes in small microwavable cup. Microwave at HIGH 30 seconds. Let stand 5 minutes to infuse flavor.

1. Combine soy sauce, lime juice, water, chili oil, garlic and ginger in medium bowl. Reserve ⅓ cup mixture for dipping sauce; set aside.

2. Cut pork tenderloin lengthwise in half; cut crosswise into 4-inch-thick slices. Cut slices into ½-inch strips. Add to bowl with soy sauce mixture; toss to coat. Cover; refrigerate at least 30 minutes or up to 2 hours, turning once.

3. To prevent sticking, spray grid with nonstick cooking spray. Prepare coals for grilling.

4. Remove pork from marinade; discard marinade. Alternately weave pork strips and thread bell pepper and onion chunks onto eight 8- to 10-inch metal skewers.

5. Grill, covered, over medium-hot coals 6 to 8 minutes or until pork is no longer pink in center, turning halfway through grilling time. Serve with rice, if desired, and reserved dipping sauce. *Makes 4 servings*

Roasted Sweet Pepper Tapas

2 red bell peppers (8 ounces each)
1 clove garlic, minced
1 teaspoon chopped fresh oregano *or* ½ teaspoon dried
oregano leaves
2 tablespoons olive oil
Garlic bread (optional)
Fresh oregano sprig for garnish

1. Cover broiler pan with foil. Adjust rack so that broiler pan is about 4 inches from heat source. Preheat broiler.

2. Place peppers on foil. Broil 15 to 20 minutes or until blackened on all sides, turning peppers every 5 minutes with tongs.

3. To steam peppers and loosen skin, place blackened peppers in paper bag. Close bag; set aside to cool about 15 to 20 minutes.

4. To peel peppers, cut around core, twist and remove. Cut peppers in half. Peel off skin. Rinse under cold water to remove seeds. Cut pepper halves into ¼-inch-wide strips.

5. Transfer pepper strips to glass jar. Add garlic, oregano and oil. Close lid; shake to blend. Marinate at least 1 hour. Serve with garlic bread, if desired, or refrigerate in jar up to 1 week. Garnish, if desired.

Makes 6 servings

Tip: Use this roasting technique for all types of sweet and hot peppers. Broiling time will vary depending on the size of the pepper. When handling hot peppers (such as Anaheims, jalapeños, poblanos or serranos) wear plastic disposable gloves and use special caution to prevent irritation of skin and eyes. Green bell peppers do not work as well, since their skins are thinner.

Shrimp Dip with Crudités

  1 can (6 ounces) cooked shrimp, drained and divided
  ½ cup reduced-fat cream cheese, softened
  ⅓ cup plus 1 tablespoon thinly sliced green onions, divided
  3 tablespoons light or fat-free Caesar salad dressing
  2 teaspoons prepared horseradish
  ¼ teaspoon salt
  2 red or yellow bell peppers, cut into 2×1-inch pieces
  4 large carrots, cut diagonally into ¼-inch-thick slices
 10 low-fat crackers

1. Reserve several shrimp for garnish. Combine remaining shrimp, cream cheese, ⅓ cup green onions, salad dressing, horseradish and salt in medium bowl; mix well. Transfer to serving dish; top with reserved shrimp and remaining 1 tablespoon green onions. Cover and chill at least 30 minutes before serving.

2. Serve with bell peppers, carrots and crackers.   *Makes 10 servings*

Herbed-Stuffed Tomatoes

 15 cherry tomatoes
  ½ cup 1% low-fat cottage cheese
  1 tablespoon thinly sliced green onion
  1 teaspoon chopped fresh chervil *or* ¼ teaspoon dried chervil
      leaves
  ½ teaspoon snipped fresh dill *or* ⅛ teaspoon dried dill weed
  ⅛ teaspoon lemon pepper

1. Cut thin slice off bottom of each tomato. Scoop out pulp with small spoon; discard pulp. Invert tomatoes onto paper towels to drain.

2. Combine cottage cheese, green onion, chervil, dill and lemon pepper in small bowl. Spoon into tomatoes. Serve at once, or cover and refrigerate up to 8 hours.   *Makes 5 servings*

Spicy Vegetable Quesadillas

Nonstick cooking spray
1 small zucchini, chopped
½ cup chopped green bell pepper
½ cup chopped onion
2 cloves garlic, minced
½ teaspoon chili powder
½ teaspoon ground cumin
8 (6-inch) flour tortillas
1 cup (4 ounces) shredded reduced-fat Cheddar cheese
¼ cup chopped fresh cilantro

1. Spray large nonstick skillet with cooking spray. Heat over medium heat until hot. Add zucchini, bell pepper, onion, garlic, chili powder and cumin; cook and stir 3 to 4 minutes or until vegetables are crisp-tender.

2. Spoon vegetable mixture evenly over half of each tortilla. Sprinkle evenly with cheese and cilantro. Fold tortillas in half.

3. Wipe skillet clean; spray skillet with cooking spray. Add tortillas and heat 1 to 2 minutes per side over medium heat or until lightly browned. Cut into thirds before serving. *Makes 8 servings*

Grilled Baby Artichokes with Pepper Dip

18 baby artichokes* (about 1½ pounds)
½ teaspoon salt
¼ cup *Frank's® RedHot®* Cayenne Pepper Sauce
¼ cup butter or margarine, melted
Roasted Pepper Dip (recipe follows)

*You can substitute 2 packages (9 ounces each) frozen artichoke halves, thawed and drained.
Do not microwave. Brush with *Frank's® RedHot®* butter mixture and grill as directed below.

1. Wash and trim tough outer leaves from artichokes. Cut ½ inch off tops of artichokes, then cut in half lengthwise. Place artichoke halves, 1 cup water and salt in 3-quart microwavable bowl. Cover; microwave on HIGH 8 minutes or until just tender. Thread artichoke halves onto metal skewers.

2. Prepare grill. Combine *Frank's RedHot* Sauce and butter in small bowl. Brush mixture over artichokes. Place artichokes on grid. Grill over hot coals 5 minutes or until tender, turning and basting often with sauce mixture. Serve artichokes with Roasted Pepper Dip. *Makes 6 servings*

Prep Time: 20 minutes
Cook Time: 13 minutes

Roasted Pepper Dip

1 jar (7 ounces) roasted red peppers, drained
1 clove garlic, chopped
¼ cup reduced-fat mayonnaise
2 tablespoons *French's®* Napa Valley Style Dijon Mustard
2 tablespoons *Frank's® RedHot®* Cayenne Pepper Sauce
¼ teaspoon salt

1. Place roasted peppers and garlic in food processor or blender. Cover; process on high until very smooth.

2. Add mayonnaise, mustard, *Frank's RedHot* Sauce and salt. Process until well blended. Cover; refrigerate 30 minutes. *Makes about 1 cup*

Prep Time: 10 minutes
Chill Time: 30 minutes

Marinated Antipasto

1 cup julienne-cut carrots
1 cup fresh green beans, cut into 2-inch pieces
1 cup fresh brussels sprouts, quartered
1 cup thinly sliced baby yellow squash
½ cup thinly sliced red bell pepper
½ cup thinly sliced yellow bell pepper
1 can (9 ounces) artichoke hearts, drained and quartered
2 cups water
½ cup white wine vinegar
1 tablespoon olive oil
1 teaspoon sugar
2 bay leaves
1 clove garlic, peeled and cut in half
6 sprigs fresh thyme
¼ teaspoon black pepper
½ cup chopped green onions with tops
½ cup minced parsley
    Peel of 2 oranges, cut into thin strips

1. Bring 4 cups water to a boil in large saucepan over high heat. Add carrots, beans and brussels sprouts; cover and simmer 1 minute. Add squash and bell peppers; cover and simmer 1 minute or until vegetables are crisp-tender. Remove from heat; drain. Place vegetables and artichoke hearts in heatproof bowl.

2. Combine 2 cups water, vinegar, oil, sugar, bay leaves, garlic, thyme and black pepper in medium saucepan. Bring to a boil over medium heat. Pour over vegetables; mix well. Cool completely. Cover and refrigerate 12 hours or up to 3 days before serving.

3. Before serving, drain vegetables. Discard bay leaves, garlic and thyme. Toss vegetables with green onions, parsley and orange peel.

Makes 8 servings

Mediterranean Phyllo Twists with Grapes and Cheese

6 sheets phyllo dough
2 tablespoons olive oil
5 to 6 ounces goat cheese
2 tablespoons chopped fresh basil
⅛ teaspoon medium-grind pepper
2 cups California seedless grapes
12 cups mixed greens
    Mustard Vinaigrette (recipe follows)
12 small California grape clusters

Cut each sheet of phyllo dough into 4 equal-size (8½×6½-inch) pieces and keep under damp, clean towel to prevent drying. Working with 4 pieces at a time, brush each piece with oil and stack, alternating directions with each piece to ensure the complete covering of filling. Portion ⅙ of cheese in center of dough. Combine basil and pepper; mix well. Top cheese with 1 teaspoon basil mixture and ⅓ cup grapes. Carefully gather dough to enclose filling, twisting dough at top to form small bundle. Brush lightly with oil to prevent drying. Place on greased baking sheet. Repeat with remaining ingredients. Bake at 400°F 10 minutes or until thoroughly heated. Toss mixed greens with Mustard Vinaigrette. Serve each phyllo packet on bed of mixed greens; garnish with grape clusters.

Makes 6 servings

Mustard Vinaigrette: Combine 3 tablespoons balsamic vinegar, 1 tablespoon *each* olive oil and chopped parsley, 1 teaspoon Dijon-style mustard, ½ teaspoon *each* sugar and salt and ¼ teaspoon pepper.

Makes ⅓ cup

Favorite recipe from *California Table Grape Commission*

Five-Layered Mexican Dip

½ cup low fat sour cream
½ cup **GUILTLESS GOURMET®** Salsa (Roasted Red Pepper or
    Southwestern Grill)
1 jar (16 ounces) **GUILTLESS GOURMET®** Black Bean Dip (Spicy or
    Mild)
2 cups shredded lettuce
½ cup chopped tomato
¼ cup (1 ounce) shredded sharp Cheddar cheese
    Chopped fresh cilantro and cilantro sprigs (optional)
1 large bag (7 ounces) **GUILTLESS GOURMET®** Baked Tortilla Chips
    (yellow, white or blue corn)

Mix together sour cream and salsa in small bowl. Spread bean dip in shallow glass bowl. Top with sour cream-salsa mixture, spreading to cover bean dip.* Just before serving, top with lettuce, tomato and cheese. Garnish with cilantro, if desired. Serve with tortilla chips.   *Makes 8 servings*

*Dip may be prepared to this point; cover and refrigerate up to 24 hours.

Coconut Chicken Tenders with Spicy Mango Salsa

1½ cups flaked coconut
1 firm ripe mango, peeled, seeded and chopped
½ cup chopped red bell pepper
3 tablespoons chopped green onion
2 tablespoons chopped fresh cilantro
  Salt
  Ground red pepper
1 egg
1 tablespoon vegetable oil
¼ teaspoon salt
  Dash ground red pepper
12 ounces chicken tenders

1. Preheat oven to 325°F. Spread coconut on large baking sheet. Bake 7 to 10 minutes or until lightly browned, stirring every 2 minutes. Transfer coconut to food processor; process until finely chopped but not pasty.

2. *Increase oven temperature to 400°F.* Combine mango, bell pepper, onion and cilantro in small bowl. Season to taste with salt and ground red pepper.

3. Transfer half of salsa to food processor; process until finely chopped (almost puréed). Combine with remaining salsa; set aside.

4. Beat egg with oil, ¼ teaspoon salt and ground red pepper in small bowl. Add chicken tenders; toss to coat. Roll tenders in coconut; arrange on foil-lined baking sheet. Bake 18 to 20 minutes or until no longer pink in center. Serve with mango salsa.   *Makes 5 to 6 servings*

Coconut Chicken Tenders
with Spicy Mango Salsa

31

Tempting
entrées

Mushroom Pasta Scampi

8 ounces uncooked linguine
2 tablespoons olive oil
1 pound fresh white mushrooms, sliced
1 tablespoon chopped garlic
1 pound frozen peeled and deveined raw large shrimp, thawed*
10 ounces fresh spinach, trimmed and torn into pieces (about 7 cups)
¼ cup grated Parmesan cheese
¼ teaspoon crushed red pepper

*To quickly thaw shrimp: Place in a colander with cold running water for about 8 minutes; drain thoroughly.

Cook linguine according to package directions. Drain, reserving ½ cup pasta water; set aside. Meanwhile, heat olive oil in large skillet. Add mushrooms and garlic; cook and stir about 5 minutes or until tender and mushroom liquid is almost evaporated. Add shrimp; cover and cook about 5 minutes or until shrimp is almost cooked through. Stir in spinach and reserved ½ cup pasta water, if desired. Cover and cook about 1 minute or until spinach is wilted. Place pasta in serving bowl; stir in mushroom and shrimp mixture, Parmesan cheese and red pepper. Toss to combine. Season with salt, if desired. *Makes 4 servings*

Favorite recipe from *Mushroom Council*

Vietnamese Loin Steaks with Black Bean Relish

1 stalk lemongrass, outer leaves removed and upper stalk trimmed
1 tablespoon sugar
1 tablespoon fish sauce
1 teaspoon minced garlic
½ to 1 teaspoon hot chili oil
2 boneless beef top loin (strip) steaks (8 ounces each)
1 can (about 9 ounces) whole baby corn, rinsed and drained
1 can (about 15 ounces) black beans, rinsed and drained
1 cup diced fresh mango
½ green bell pepper, cut into strips
2 tablespoons chopped red onion
1 jalapeño pepper,* seeded and thinly sliced (optional)
Juice of ½ lemon
½ teaspoon vegetable oil
½ teaspoon honey
⅛ teaspoon salt

*Jalapeños can sting and irritate the skin; wear rubber gloves when handling and do not touch eyes. Wash hands after handling peppers.

1. Flatten lemongrass with meat mallet and mince. Combine with sugar, fish sauce, garlic and chili oil in baking dish. Cut each steak lengthwise into 2 strips. Place in dish with marinade, coating both sides. Cover; refrigerate 1 hour, turning once.

2. Halve corn cobs diagonally; combine with beans, mango, bell pepper, onion and jalapeño pepper, if desired, in large bowl. Combine lemon juice, oil, honey and salt in small bowl; stir into bean mixture.

3. Grill steaks over medium heat, uncovered, 10 to 12 minutes for medium-rare to medium or until desired doneness, turning once. Serve with relish.

Makes 4 servings

**Vietnamese Loin Steak
with Black Bean Relish**

Pesto Chicken & Pepper Wraps

⅔ cup refrigerated pesto sauce or frozen pesto sauce, thawed and divided
3 tablespoons red wine vinegar
¼ teaspoon salt
¼ teaspoon black pepper
1¼ pounds skinless boneless chicken thighs or breasts
2 red bell peppers, cut in half, stemmed and seeded
5 (8-inch) flour tortillas
5 thin slices (3-inch rounds) fresh-pack mozzarella cheese*
5 leaves Boston or red leaf lettuce
  Orange slices
  Red and green chilies
  Fresh basil sprigs

*Packaged sliced whole milk or part-skim mozzarella cheese can be substituted for fresh-pack mozzarella cheese.

Combine ¼ cup pesto, vinegar, salt and black pepper in medium bowl. Add chicken; toss to coat. Cover and refrigerate at least 30 minutes. Remove chicken from marinade; discard marinade. Grill chicken over medium-hot KINGSFORD® Briquets about 4 minutes per side until chicken is no longer pink in center, turning once. Grill bell peppers, skin sides down, about 8 minutes until skin is charred. Place bell peppers in large resealable plastic food storage bag; seal. Let stand 5 minutes; remove skin. Cut chicken and bell peppers into thin strips. Spread about 1 tablespoon of remaining pesto down center of each tortilla; top with chicken, bell peppers, cheese and lettuce. Roll tortillas to enclose filling. Garnish with orange slices, chilies and basil sprigs.   *Makes 5 wraps*

Teriyaki Salmon with Asian Slaw

4 tablespoons light teriyaki sauce, divided
2 (5- to 6-ounce) boneless salmon fillets with skin (1 inch thick)
2½ cups packaged coleslaw mix
1 cup fresh pea pods, cut lengthwise into thin strips
½ cup thinly sliced radishes
2 tablespoons orange marmalade
1 teaspoon sesame oil

1. Preheat broiler or prepare grill. Spoon 2 tablespoons teriyaki sauce over meaty sides of salmon. Let stand while preparing vegetable mixture.

2. Combine coleslaw mix, pea pods and radishes in large bowl. Combine remaining 2 tablespoons teriyaki sauce, marmalade and sesame oil in small bowl. Add to cabbage mixture; toss well.

3. Broil salmon 4 to 5 inches from heat source, or grill over medium coals, without turning, 6 to 10 minutes or until center is opaque.

4. Transfer cabbage mixture to serving plates; top with salmon.

Makes 2 servings

Fresh Tip

Packaged coleslaw mix makes for speedy preparation of this Asian inspired meal. Choose a coleslaw mix with both green and red cabbage for a colorful presentation.

Caramelized Onion & Eggplant Sandwiches

Grilled Garlic Aioli (recipe follows) or mayonnaise
½ cup packed brown sugar
½ cup water
½ cup soy sauce
2 tablespoons molasses
5 slices fresh ginger
¼ teaspoon ground coriander
Dash black pepper
1 large yellow onion
4 large eggplant slices, 1 inch thick
4 round buns, split
4 tomato slices
Mixed greens
Radishes
Carrot curls

Prepare Grilled Garlic Aioli; set aside. Combine sugar, water, soy sauce, molasses, ginger, coriander and pepper in small saucepan. Bring to boil, stirring constantly. Reduce heat; simmer marinade 5 minutes, stirring occasionally. Cool. Cut onion into ½-inch-thick slices. Insert wooden picks into onion slices from edges to prevent separating into rings. (Soak wooden picks in hot water 15 minutes to prevent burning.) Marinate eggplant and onion in marinade 10 to 15 minutes. Remove vegetables from marinade; reserve marinade. Lightly oil grid to prevent sticking. Grill vegetables on covered grill around edge of medium-hot KINGSFORD® Briquets about 20 minutes or until tender, turning once or twice and brushing with reserved marinade. Place buns on grill, cut sides down, until toasted. Serve eggplant and onion on grilled buns with tomato, greens and Grilled Garlic Aioli. Garnish with radishes and carrot curls.   *Makes 4 sandwiches*

Grilled Garlic Aioli: Prepare Grilled Garlic (recipe follows). Mash 8 cloves Grilled Garlic in small bowl. Add ¼ cup mayonnaise; mix until blended.

Grilled Garlic: Peel outermost papery skin from 1 or 2 garlic heads. Brush garlic with olive oil. Grill at edge of grid on covered grill over medium-hot Kingsford® Briquets 30 to 45 minutes or until cloves are soft and buttery. Remove from grill; cool slightly. Gently squeeze softened garlic head from root end so that cloves slip out of skins into small bowl. Use immediately or cover and refrigerate up to 1 week.

Pepper Stuffed Flank Steak with Chef's Signature Steak Sauce

1 flank steak (about 1½ pounds)
Salt
Ground black pepper
2 cups thinly sliced bell peppers (green, red and/or yellow)
1 small onion, thinly sliced
Chef's Signature Steak Sauce (recipe follows)

Lay steak flat on baking sheet lined with plastic wrap. Cover and freeze about 2 hours or until nearly firm. Place steak on cutting board. Hold large sharp knife parallel to steak. Carefully cut steak in half lengthwise. Thaw in refrigerator until steak can be rolled up easily. Sprinkle inside of each piece of meat with salt and black pepper. Arrange bell peppers and onion on meat, leaving ½-inch edge around meat. Tightly roll up jelly-roll style; tie with kitchen string or secure with toothpicks. (Soak toothpicks in water 20 minutes before using, to prevent burning.)

Prepare Chef's Signature Steak Sauce; set aside. Place steak on oiled grid. Grill over medium-hot coals 25 minutes for medium doneness, turning often. Baste with some of Chef's Signature Steak Sauce during last 10 minutes of cooking. Remove string or toothpicks. Let stand 5 minutes. Slice diagonally. Serve with remaining sauce.   *Makes 6 servings*

Chef's Signature Steak Sauce

½ cup ketchup
¼ cup *French's®* Worcestershire Sauce
1 to 2 tablespoons *Frank's® RedHot®* Cayenne Pepper Sauce
2 cloves garlic, minced

Combine ingredients in small bowl; stir until smooth.   *Makes ¾ cup*

Prep Time: 30 minutes
Freeze Time: 2 hours
Cook Time: 25 minutes

Sesame Chicken and Vegetable Stir-Fry

1 tablespoon dark sesame oil
1 pound chicken tenders, cut into 1-inch pieces
2 cups broccoli florets
1 small red bell pepper, sliced
½ cup onion slices (about 1 small)
½ cup snow peas
1 can (8 ounces) sliced water chestnuts, drained
2 cloves garlic, minced
1 teaspoon Chinese five-spice powder
1 cup fat-free reduced-sodium chicken broth
2 teaspoons cornstarch
2 tablespoons cold water
2 cups hot cooked rice

1. Heat sesame oil in wok or large nonstick skillet over medium heat until hot. Add chicken; stir-fry about 8 minutes or until chicken is no longer pink in center. Remove chicken from wok.

2. Add broccoli, bell pepper, onion, snow peas, water chestnuts and garlic to wok; stir-fry 5 to 8 minutes or until vegetables are crisp-tender. Sprinkle with five-spice powder; cook and stir 1 minute.

3. Return chicken to wok. Add chicken broth; heat to a boil. Combine cornstarch and water in small bowl; stir into broth mixture. Boil 1 to 2 minutes, stirring constantly. Serve over rice. *Makes 4 servings*

Tempting entrées

Fiery Grilled Buffalo-Style Chops and Vegetables

Zesty Blue Cheese Butter (recipe follows)
4 medium baking potatoes, unpeeled
Vegetable oil
4 (¾-inch-thick) boneless pork loin chops (about 4 ounces each)
2 medium red bell peppers, cut into halves and seeded
⅓ cup butter or margarine
⅓ cup hot pepper sauce
Prepared coleslaw (optional)

1. Prepare Zesty Blue Cheese Butter up to 2 days in advance; refrigerate.

2. Preheat oven to 375°F. Scrub potatoes. Pierce each potato several times with fork. Pat potatoes dry with paper towels; rub skins with oil. Bake 1 hour or until just fork-tender. While hot, cut potatoes lengthwise in half. Cool to room temperature.

3. Prepare grill for direct cooking.

4. Place pork chops, bell peppers and potatoes in large resealable plastic food storage bag. Melt butter in small saucepan over low heat. Stir in pepper sauce; pour over chops, bell peppers and potatoes. Seal bag tightly; turn to coat. Marinate at room temperature no more than 15 minutes, turning once.

5. Place chops and vegetables on grid, reserving marinade in small saucepan. Grill, uncovered, over medium coals 5 minutes. Turn chops and vegetables and baste once with reserved marinade; discard any remaining marinade. Grill 5 minutes more or until pork is barely pink in center. (Do not overcook.)

6. Serve chops and vegetables with slices of Zesty Blue Cheese Butter.

Makes 4 servings

Zesty Blue Cheese Butter

4 ounces blue cheese, such as Gorgonzola or Roquefort
½ cup butter or margarine, softened
1 package (3 ounces) cream cheese, softened
2 tablespoons finely chopped green onion
2 slices bacon, crisp-cooked, drained and crumbled

1. Crumble blue cheese with fingers to measure 1 cup; place in small bowl.

2. Add butter and cream cheese; beat with electric mixer at medium speed until smooth. Stir in onion and bacon.

3. Place butter mixture on sheet of waxed paper. Using waxed paper, roll mixture back and forth into 8-inch log.

4. Wrap waxed paper around butter log to seal. Refrigerate at least 1 hour or up to 2 days.

Makes about 1 cup

Grilled Fish with Orange-Chile Salsa

3 medium oranges, peeled and sectioned* (about 1¼ cups segments)
¼ cup finely diced green, red or yellow bell pepper
3 tablespoons chopped cilantro, divided
3 tablespoons lime juice, divided
1 tablespoon honey
1 teaspoon minced, seeded serrano pepper** *or* 1 tablespoon minced jalapeño pepper
1¼ pounds firm white fish fillets, such as orange roughy, lingcod, halibut or red snapper
Lime slices
Zucchini ribbons, cooked

*Canned mandarin orange segments can be substituted for fresh orange segments, if desired.

**Hot peppers can sting and irritate the skin; wear rubber gloves when handling and do not touch your eyes. Wash hands after handling peppers.

To prepare Orange-Chile Salsa, combine orange segments, bell pepper, 2 tablespoons cilantro, 2 tablespoons lime juice, honey and serrano pepper. Set aside.

Season fish fillets with remaining 1 tablespoon cilantro and 1 tablespoon lime juice. Lightly oil grid to prevent sticking. Grill fish on covered grill over medium KINGSFORD® Briquets 5 minutes. Turn and top with lime slices, if desired. Grill about 5 minutes until fish flakes easily when tested with fork. Serve with Orange-Chile Salsa. Garnish with zucchini ribbons.

Makes 4 servings

Note: Allow about 10 minutes grilling time per inch thickness of fish fillets.

Thai Curry Stir-Fry

½ cup fat-free reduced-sodium chicken broth
2 teaspoons cornstarch
2 teaspoons reduced-sodium soy sauce
1½ teaspoons curry powder
⅛ teaspoon red pepper flakes
   Nonstick olive oil cooking spray
3 green onions, sliced
2 cloves garlic, minced
2 cups broccoli florets
⅔ cup sliced carrot
1½ teaspoons olive oil
6 ounces boneless skinless chicken breast, cut into bite-size pieces
⅔ cup hot cooked rice, prepared without salt

1. Stir together broth, cornstarch, soy sauce, curry powder and red pepper; set aside.

2. Spray nonstick wok or large nonstick skillet with cooking spray. Heat over medium-high heat. Add onions and garlic; stir-fry 1 minute. Remove from wok.

3. Add broccoli and carrot to wok; stir-fry 2 to 3 minutes or until crisp-tender. Remove from wok.

4. Add oil to hot wok. Add chicken and stir-fry 2 to 3 minutes or until no longer pink. Stir broth mixture. Add to wok. Cook and stir until broth mixture comes to a boil and thickens slightly. Return all vegetables to wok; heat through.

5. Serve chicken mixture over rice.

Makes 2 servings

Hickory Beef Kabobs

1 pound boneless beef top sirloin or tenderloin steaks, cut into
   1¼-inch pieces
2 ears fresh corn, shucked, cleaned and cut crosswise into 1-inch
   pieces
1 red or green bell pepper, cut into 1-inch squares
1 small red onion, cut into ½-inch wedges
½ cup beer
½ cup chili sauce
1 teaspoon dry mustard
2 cloves garlic, minced
3 cups hot cooked white rice
¼ cup chopped fresh parsley

1. Place beef, corn, bell pepper and onion in large resealable plastic food storage bag. Combine beer, chili sauce, mustard and garlic in small bowl; pour over beef and vegetables. Seal bag tightly, turning to coat. Marinate in refrigerator at least 1 hour or up to 8 hours, turning occasionally.

2. Prepare grill for direct cooking. Meanwhile, cover 1½ cups hickory chips with cold water; soak 20 minutes.

3. Drain beef and vegetables; reserve marinade. Alternately thread beef and vegetables onto 4 (12-inch) metal skewers. Brush with reserved marinade.

4. Drain hickory chips; sprinkle over coals. Place kabobs on grid. Grill kabobs, uncovered, over medium heat 5 minutes. Brush with reserved marinade; turn and brush again. Discard remaining marinade. Continue to grill 5 to 7 minutes for medium or until desired doneness.

5. Combine rice and chopped parsley; serve kabobs over rice mixture.

Makes 4 servings

Chicken Primavera Buffet

     Nonstick cooking spray
 12 ounces uncooked thin spaghetti
 ¼ cup prepared pesto
 ¼ cup prepared fat-free Italian salad dressing
 ½ teaspoon red pepper flakes
  2 cups water
  1 cup thinly sliced carrots
  1 cup broccoli florets
  1 cup snow peas
  1 can (4 ounces) sliced water chestnuts, drained
  8 boneless skinless chicken breasts

1. Preheat oven to 350°F. Spray 13×9-inch baking dish with cooking spray. Cook pasta according to package directions, omitting salt. Drain and rinse well under cold water until pasta is cool; drain well. Place in large bowl; set aside.

2. Combine pesto, Italian dressing and red pepper flakes in small bowl. Reserve 1 tablespoon pesto mixture. Add remaining pesto mixture to pasta; toss to coat well.

3. In large saucepan, bring water to a boil over high heat. Add carrots, broccoli and snow peas; cook 3 minutes. Drain vegetables. Add water chestnuts and vegetables to pasta; toss to blend well. Transfer pasta and vegetables to prepared dish.

4. Spray large nonstick skillet with cooking spray; heat over medium heat until hot. Add chicken; cook until browned on both sides. Cover; cook 10 minutes or until no longer pink in center and juices run clear. Place chicken on pasta and vegetables. Pour juices from skillet over chicken. Spread reserved pesto mixture over chicken. Bake 45 minutes or until heated through. *Makes 8 servings*

Tempting entrées

Glazed Stuffed Pork Chops

2 medium baking apples
Lemon juice
3 cups prepared cabbage slaw blend
¼ cup raisins
¾ cup apple cider, divided
2 tablespoons maple-flavored pancake syrup
4 teaspoons spicy brown mustard, divided
2 lean bone-in pork chops, 1 inch thick (about 6 ounces each)
Nonstick cooking spray
2 teaspoons cornstarch

1. Quarter and core apples. Chop 6 quarters. Reserve remaining 2 quarters for garnish (sprinkle with lemon juice to prevent browning). Combine chopped apples, slaw blend, raisins, ¼ cup apple cider, syrup and 2 teaspoons mustard in large saucepan. Cover and cook over medium heat 5 minutes or until cabbage is tender.

2. Make a pocket in each pork chop by cutting horizontally through chop almost to bone. Fill each pocket with about ¼ cup cabbage mixture. Keep remaining cabbage mixture warm over low heat.

3. Spray medium nonstick skillet with cooking spray; heat over medium heat until hot. Brown pork chops about 3 minutes on each side. Add ¼ cup apple cider. Reduce heat to low; cover and cook 8 minutes or until pork is barely pink in center. Remove pork from skillet; keep warm.

4. Add liquid from remaining cabbage mixture to skillet. Combine remaining ¼ cup cider, 2 teaspoons mustard and cornstarch in small bowl until smooth. Stir into liquid in skillet. Simmer over medium heat until thickened.

5. Spoon glaze over chops and cabbage mixture. Slice remaining 2 apple quarters; divide between servings. *Makes 2 servings*

Skillet Chicken with California Asparagus

4 boneless skinless chicken breast halves (1 pound)
Paprika
1 teaspoon vegetable oil
½ teaspoon sesame oil
1 cup plus 2 tablespoons reduced-sodium chicken broth, divided
1 medium onion, sliced
1 medium clove garlic, minced
1 tablespoon chopped fresh dill *or* 1 teaspoon dried dill weed
1 pound fresh California asparagus
Boiling water
1 tablespoon cornstarch
1 jar (2 ounces) sliced pimientos, drained
1 cup uncooked orzo pasta, cooked (about 3 cups)

Rinse chicken breasts and pat dry; remove any excess fat. Lightly sprinkle chicken with paprika. In large nonstick skillet sprayed with nonstick cooking spray, heat oils. Quickly brown chicken on both sides, over medium-high heat, about 5 minutes. Reduce heat; add 1 cup broth, onion, garlic and dill. Cover; simmer 10 to 12 minutes or until chicken is tender.

Meanwhile, trim or break off asparagus spears at tender point; rinse. In large skillet, in boiling water to cover, cook asparagus until crisp-tender, about 3 to 5 minutes. *Do not overcook.* Drain and rinse under cold water.

Combine cornstarch with remaining 2 tablespoons chicken broth; stir into chicken mixture. Add pimientos. Cook, stirring, until sauce thickens. On 4 individual plates or serving platter, arrange chicken breasts on hot cooked pasta. Add asparagus spears to sauce in skillet; heat briefly. Arrange asparagus on plates and serve sauce over chicken, pasta and asparagus. Garnish with fresh dill, if desired. *Makes 4 servings*

Favorite recipe from *California Asparagus Commission*

Grilled Salmon Salad with Orange-Basil Vinaigrette

¼ cup frozen orange juice concentrate, thawed
1 tablespoon plus 1½ teaspoons white wine vinegar or cider vinegar
1 tablespoon chopped fresh basil
1½ teaspoons olive oil
1 (8-ounce) salmon fillet (about 1 inch thick)
4 cups torn mixed greens
¾ cup sliced strawberries
10 to 12 thin cucumber slices, cut into halves
⅛ teaspoon coarsely ground black pepper

1. Whisk together orange juice concentrate, vinegar, basil and olive oil. Set aside 2 tablespoons juice concentrate mixture. Reserve remaining mixture to use as salad dressing.

2. Prepare grill for direct grilling. Grill salmon, skin side down, over medium coals 5 minutes. Turn and grill 5 minutes or until fish flakes easily when tested with fork, brushing frequently with 2 tablespoons juice concentrate mixture. Cool slightly.

3. Toss together greens, strawberries and cucumber slices. Divide evenly between two serving plates.

4. Remove skin from salmon. Break salmon into chunks. Arrange salmon on greens mixture. Drizzle with reserved juice concentrate mixture. Sprinkle with pepper.

Makes 2 servings

Grilled Salmon Salad
with Orange-Basil Vinaigrette

59

Korean-Style Beef and Pasta

1 beef top round steak (about ¾ pound)
2 tablespoons reduced-sodium soy sauce
1 tablespoon rice wine
2 teaspoons sugar
  Korean-Style Dressing (recipe follows)
1 package (about 7 ounces) uncooked rice noodles
2 cups thinly sliced napa cabbage
1¾ cups thinly sliced yellow bell peppers
½ cup thinly sliced radishes
1 medium carrot, shredded
2 green onions, thinly sliced

1. Freeze beef until partially firm; cut into very thin slices.

2. Combine soy sauce, rice wine and sugar in small nonmetallic bowl. Add beef slices; toss to coat evenly. Cover and refrigerate 8 hours or overnight.

3. Drain beef; discard marinade. Grill beef over medium-hot coals 2 to 3 minutes or until desired doneness.

4. Meanwhile, prepare Korean-Style Dressing; set aside.

5. Cook noodles in boiling water 1 to 2 minutes or until tender; drain and rinse under cold water. Arrange noodles on platter.

6. Combine cabbage, bell peppers, radishes, carrot, green onions and beef in medium bowl. Add Korean-Style Dressing; toss to coat evenly. Serve over noodles. Garnish with green onion brush and carrot ribbons, if desired.

Makes 6 to 8 servings

Tempting entrées

Korean-Style Dressing

  2 teaspoons sesame seeds
⅓ cup orange juice
  2 tablespoons rice wine
  2 teaspoons reduced-sodium soy sauce
  1 teaspoon dark sesame oil
  1 teaspoon grated fresh ginger
  1 teaspoon sugar
  1 clove garlic, minced
⅛ teaspoon red pepper flakes

1. Place sesame seeds in small nonstick skillet. Cook and stir over medium heat until lightly browned and toasted, about 5 minutes. Cool completely.

2. Crush sesame seeds, using mortar and pestle or wooden spoon; transfer to small bowl.

3. Add orange juice, rice wine, soy sauce, sesame oil, ginger, sugar, garlic and red pepper flakes. Blend well.

Jamaican Pork and Mango Stir-Fry

1 pork tenderloin (about 1 pound)
2 tablespoons olive oil
1 tablespoon Caribbean jerk seasoning blend
1 medium mango, peeled and chopped *or* ½ (26-ounce) jar mango
    slices in light syrup, drained and chopped
1 red bell pepper, chopped
⅔ cup orange juice
2 teaspoons cornstarch
½ teaspoon jalapeño pepper sauce *or* ¼ teaspoon hot pepper sauce
¼ cup sliced green onions

1. Trim fat from pork and discard. Cut pork into thin strips.

2. Heat oil in large skillet or wok over medium-high heat until hot. Add pork and seasoning blend; stir-fry 2 minutes. Add mango and bell pepper; stir-fry 2 minutes or just until pork is no longer pink.

3. Blend orange juice, cornstarch and pepper sauce in small bowl until smooth; add to skillet. Cook and stir 2 minutes or until sauce is clear and thickened. Stir in green onions. *Makes 4 servings*

Serving Suggestion: Create an easy island side salad by adding canned pineapple tidbits and raisins to prepared coleslaw.

Tip: Look for firm, but not hard, mangoes with a yellow or red blush. Underripe fruit can be ripened in a paper bag for 1 to 3 days. Ripe mangoes have a sweet, fruity aroma.

Prep and Cook Time: 17 minutes

Sesame Peanut Spaghetti Squash

1 spaghetti squash (3 pounds)
⅓ cup sesame seeds
⅓ cup vegetable broth
2 tablespoons reduced-sodium soy sauce
1 tablespoon sugar
2 teaspoons sesame oil
1 teaspoon cornstarch
1 teaspoon red pepper flakes
1 teaspoon Worcestershire sauce
1 tablespoon vegetable oil
2 medium carrots, julienned
1 large red bell pepper, seeded and thinly sliced
¼ pound fresh snow peas, cut diagonally in half
½ cup coarsely chopped unsalted peanuts
⅓ cup minced fresh cilantro

1. Preheat oven to 350°F. Spray 13×9-inch baking dish with nonstick cooking spray. Wash squash; cut in half lengthwise. Remove and discard seeds. Place squash, cut side down, in prepared dish. Bake 45 minutes to 1 hour or until just tender.

2. Using fork, remove strands from hot squash and place in large bowl. (Use oven mitts to protect hands.) Cover and keep warm.

3. To toast sesame seeds, heat wok over medium-high heat until hot. Add sesame seeds; cook and stir 45 seconds or until golden brown. Remove to blender. Add broth, soy sauce, sugar, sesame oil, cornstarch, red pepper flakes and Worcestershire sauce. Process until mixture is coarsely puréed.

4. Heat wok or large skillet over medium-high heat 1 minute or until hot. Drizzle vegetable oil into wok; heat 30 seconds. Add carrots; stir-fry 1 minute. Add bell pepper; stir-fry 2 minutes or until vegetables are crisp-tender. Add snow peas; stir-fry 1 minute. Stir sesame seed mixture; add to wok. Cook and stir 1 minute or until sauce is thickened.

5. Pour vegetable mixture over spaghetti squash. Add peanuts and cilantro; toss well, if desired. *Makes 4 servings*

Curried Chicken & Potato Wraps

    Mango Salsa (recipe follows)
  6 (8-inch) fat-free flour tortillas
    Nonstick cooking spray
  1 medium onion, chopped
  2 tablespoons minced fresh ginger
  2 tablespoons minced garlic (10 to 12 cloves)
 12 ounces boneless skinless chicken thighs, cut into 1-inch pieces
  1 tablespoon curry powder
 ¼ teaspoon ground red pepper
  1 can (about 14 ounces) fat-free reduced-sodium chicken broth
  2 large potatoes (about 1 pound), peeled and cut into ½-inch cubes
 ½ cup raisins
 ¼ cup cider vinegar
  2 tablespoons brown sugar
 ¼ cup chopped fresh cilantro

1. Prepare Mango Salsa. Wrap flour tortillas in plastic; set aside.

2. Spray large nonstick skillet with cooking spray; heat over high heat. Add onion, ginger and garlic; cook and stir 4 minutes or until onion is crisp-tender and golden. Add chicken; cook, without stirring, 4 minutes or until golden. Turn chicken; cook 2 minutes more.

3. Add curry powder and red pepper to skillet; cook and stir 30 seconds or until fragrant. Stir in chicken broth, potatoes, raisins, vinegar and brown sugar; bring to a boil. Reduce heat to low; partially cover and simmer 30 minutes or until potatoes are tender when pierced. Uncover; simmer, while gently stirring, until most liquid is absorbed. Remove from heat; stir in cilantro.

4. Place tortillas in microwave and microwave at HIGH 1 to 2 minutes or until pliable. Spoon chicken mixture onto center of tortillas. Top with Mango Salsa. Fold all 4 sides of tortillas over filling. *Makes 6 servings*

Mango Salsa

1 large ripe mango, peeled and cubed
3 tablespoons lime juice
2 tablespoons minced fresh cilantro or fresh mint leaves

Combine all ingredients in small bowl.

Makes about 1 cup

Grilled Tropical Shrimp

¼ **cup prepared barbecue sauce**
2 **tablespoons pineapple juice or orange juice**
10 **ounces raw medium shrimp in shells**
2 **medium nectarines**
1 **yellow onion, cut into 8 wedges** *or* **6 green onions, cut into
2-inch lengths**

1. Stir together barbecue sauce and pineapple juice; set aside.

2. Peel and devein shrimp. Cut each nectarine into 6 wedges. Thread shrimp, nectarines and onion wedges onto 4 long metal skewers.

3. Spray grill grid with nonstick cooking spray. Prepare grill for direct grilling. Grill skewers over medium coals 4 to 5 minutes or until shrimp are opaque, turning once and brushing frequently with barbecue sauce.

Makes 2 servings

Fresh Tip

Choose firm but not hard nectarines for this recipe. If nectarines are too soft, they will fall off the skewers during grilling.

Seafood & Vegetable Stir-Fry

  2 teaspoons olive oil
  ½ medium red or yellow bell pepper, cut into strips
  ½ medium onion, cut into small wedges
 10 snow peas, trimmed and cut diagonally into halves
  1 clove garlic, minced
  6 ounces frozen cooked medium shrimp, thawed
  2 tablespoons stir-fry sauce
  1 cup hot cooked rice

1. Heat oil in large nonstick skillet over medium-high heat. Add vegetables; stir-fry 4 minutes. Add garlic; stir fry 1 minute or until vegetables are crisp-tender.

2. Add shrimp and stir-fry sauce. Stir-fry 1 to 2 minutes or until hot. Serve over rice. *Makes 2 servings*

Hidden Valley® Wraps

  1 cup HIDDEN VALLEY® The Original Ranch® Dressing
  1 package (8 ounces) cream cheese, softened
 10 ounces sliced turkey breast
 10 ounces Monterey Jack cheese slices
  2 large avocados, peeled and thinly sliced
  2 medium tomatoes, thinly sliced
    Shredded lettuce
  4 (12-inch) flour tortillas, warmed

Beat together dressing and cream cheese. Evenly layer ¼ of turkey, Monterey Jack cheese, dressing mixture, avocados, tomatoes and lettuce among tortillas, leaving a 1-inch border around edges. Repeat layering with remaining ingredients. Fold right and left edges of tortillas into centers over the filling. Fold the bottom edge toward the center and roll firmly until completely wrapped. Place seam side down and cut in half diagonally. *Makes 4 servings*

Soups & stews

Beef and Parsnip Stew

1¼ pounds beef stew meat, cut into ¾-inch cubes
½ cup all-purpose flour
2 tablespoons vegetable oil
4½ cups canned beef broth
½ cup dry red wine
1 teaspoon salt
½ teaspoon dried Italian seasoning
⅛ teaspoon black pepper
8 ounces peeled baby carrots
2 parsnips, peeled and cut into ⅜-inch slices
¾ cup sugar snap peas

1. Toss beef in flour to coat. Heat oil in large saucepan over medium-high heat. Add beef and remaining flour; brown, stirring frequently.

2. Stir in broth, wine, salt, Italian seasoning and pepper. Bring to a boil over high heat. Reduce heat to medium-low; simmer, uncovered, 1 hour.

3. Add carrots; cook 15 minutes. Add parsnips; simmer 8 minutes or until vegetables and meat are tender. Stir in peas. Cook and stir over medium heat until heated through. *Makes 5 servings*

Shrimp Étouffée

  3 tablespoons vegetable oil
¼ cup all-purpose flour
  1 cup chopped onion
  1 cup chopped green bell pepper
½ cup chopped carrots
½ cup chopped celery
  4 cloves garlic, minced
  1 can (14½ ounces) clear vegetable broth
  1 bottle (8 ounces) clam juice
½ teaspoon salt
2½ pounds raw large shrimp, peeled and deveined
  1 teaspoon red pepper flakes
  1 teaspoon hot pepper sauce
  4 cups hot cooked white or basmati rice
½ cup chopped flat-leaf parsley

1. Heat oil in Dutch oven over medium heat. Add flour; cook and stir 10 to 15 minutes or until flour mixture is deep golden brown. Add onion, bell pepper, carrots, celery and garlic; cook and stir 5 minutes.

2. Stir in broth, clam juice and salt; bring to a boil. Simmer, uncovered, 10 minutes or until vegetables are tender. Stir in shrimp, red pepper flakes and pepper sauce; simmer 6 to 8 minutes or until shrimp are opaque.

3. Ladle into eight shallow bowls; top each with ½ cup rice. Sprinkle with parsley. Serve with additional pepper sauce, if desired.

Makes 8 servings

Greens, White Bean and Barley Soup

½ pound carrots, peeled
2 tablespoons olive oil
1½ cups chopped onions
2 cloves garlic, minced
1½ cups sliced button mushrooms
6 cups vegetable broth
2 cups cooked barley
1 can (16 ounces) Great Northern beans, rinsed and drained
2 bay leaves
1 teaspoon sugar
1 teaspoon dried thyme leaves
1½ pounds collard greens, washed, stemmed and chopped (about 7 cups)
1 tablespoon white wine vinegar
Hot pepper sauce
Red bell pepper strips for garnish (optional)

1. Cut carrots lengthwise into quarters; cut crosswise into ¼-inch pieces.

2. Heat oil in Dutch oven over medium heat until hot. Add carrots, onions and garlic; cook and stir 3 minutes. Add mushrooms; cook and stir 5 minutes or until tender.

3. Add broth, barley, beans, bay leaves, sugar and thyme. Bring to a boil over high heat. Reduce heat to low. Cover and simmer 5 minutes.

4. Add greens; simmer 10 minutes.

5. Remove bay leaves; discard. Stir in vinegar. Season to taste with pepper sauce. Garnish, if desired.   *Makes 8 (1¼-cup) servings*

Chicken and Sweet Potato Ragoût

2 tablespoons vegetable oil, divided
1 (3-pound) chicken, cut into 8 pieces
1 large onion, chopped
1 (14½-ounce) can chicken broth
3 small sweet potatoes, peeled and cut into ¼-inch slices
2 cups shredded green cabbage
1 tablespoon TABASCO® brand Pepper Sauce
1 teaspoon salt
¼ cup water
1 tablespoon flour
¼ cup peanut butter

Heat 1 tablespoon oil in 12-inch skillet over medium heat. Add chicken; cook until well browned. Remove to plate. Add remaining 1 tablespoon oil and onion to skillet; cook 5 minutes. Return chicken to skillet; add broth, potatoes, cabbage, TABASCO® Sauce and salt. Heat to boiling over high heat. Reduce heat to low; cover and simmer 30 minutes or until tender, stirring occasionally.

Combine water and flour in small cup. Gradually stir into skillet with peanut butter. Cook over high heat until mixture thickens.

Makes 4 servings

Cheesy Polenta with Zucchini Stew

2¼ cups water, divided
1 cup stone-ground or regular yellow cornmeal
2 eggs
2 egg whites
¾ cup (3 ounces) reduced-fat sharp Cheddar cheese
1 jalapeño pepper,* minced
1 teaspoon margarine
½ teaspoon salt, divided
1 tablespoon olive oil
2 cups coarsely chopped peeled eggplant
1 cup chopped onion
3 cloves minced garlic
3 cups chopped zucchini
1 cup chopped tomatoes
½ cup chopped yellow bell pepper
2 tablespoons minced fresh parsley
1 tablespoon minced fresh oregano
¼ teaspoon minced fresh rosemary
¼ teaspoon red pepper flakes
¼ teaspoon ground pepper blend

*Jalapeño peppers can sting and irritate the skin; wear rubber gloves when handling peppers and do not touch eyes. Wash hands after handling peppers.

1. Bring 2 cups water to a boil. Slowly add cornmeal, stirring constantly. Bring to a boil, stirring constantly, until mixture thickens. Lightly beat eggs and egg whites with remaining ¼ cup water. Add to cornmeal; cook and stir until bubbly. Remove from heat; stir in cheese, jalapeño pepper, margarine and ¼ teaspoon salt. Pour into 9-inch square baking pan. Cover and refrigerate several hours or until firm.

2. Heat olive oil in medium saucepan over medium heat until hot. Cook and stir eggplant, onion and garlic 5 minutes or until onion is transparent. Add zucchini, tomatoes, bell pepper, parsley, oregano, remaining ¼ teaspoon salt, rosemary, red pepper flakes and pepper blend. Simmer, uncovered, 1 hour.

3. Spray large nonstick skillet with nonstick vegetable cooking spray. Heat skillet over medium heat until hot. Cut polenta into 6 rectangles. Cook over medium heat 8 minutes on each side or until crusty and lightly browned. Serve zucchini stew over polenta.   *Makes 6 servings*

Thai Noodle Soup

1 package (3 ounces) ramen noodles, uncooked
12 ounces chicken tenders
2 cans (about 14 ounces each) chicken broth
¼ cup shredded carrot
¼ cup frozen snow peas
2 tablespoons thinly sliced green onion tops
½ teaspoon minced garlic
¼ teaspoon ground ginger
3 tablespoons chopped fresh cilantro
½ lime, cut into 4 wedges

1. Break noodles into pieces. Cook noodles according to package directions, discarding flavor packet. Drain and set aside.

2. Cut chicken tenders into ½-inch pieces. Combine chicken broth and chicken tenders in large saucepan or Dutch oven; bring to a boil over medium heat. Cook 2 minutes.

3. Add carrot, snow peas, green onion tops, garlic and ginger. Reduce heat to low; simmer 3 minutes.

4. Add cooked noodles and cilantro; heat through. Serve soup with lime wedges.   *Makes 4 servings*

Prep and Cook Time: 15 minutes

Creamy Crab Chowder

1 tablespoon butter or margarine
1 cup finely chopped onion
2 cloves garlic, minced
1 cup finely chopped celery
½ cup finely chopped green bell pepper
½ cup finely chopped red bell pepper
3 cans (about 14 ounces each) chicken broth
3 cups diced peeled potatoes
1 package (10 ounces) frozen corn
2 cans (6½ ounces each) lump crabmeat
½ cup half-and-half
¼ teaspoon black pepper

1. Melt butter over medium heat in Dutch oven. Add onion and garlic. Cook and stir 6 minutes or until softened but not browned.

2. Add celery and bell peppers. Cook 8 minutes or until celery is tender, stirring often.

3. Add broth and potatoes. Bring to a boil over high heat. Reduce heat to low and simmer 10 minutes. Add corn; cook 5 minutes or until potatoes are tender.

4. Drain crabmeat and place in small bowl. Flake to break up large pieces; add to Dutch oven. Stir in half-and-half and black pepper. Bring to a simmer. *Do not boil.* Serve hot.   *Makes 6 to 8 servings*

Tuscan-Style Lamb with White Beans

- 1 pound large dried lima (butter) beans
- 2 tablespoons Lucini Premium Select extra virgin olive oil
- 3 pounds lamb shoulder, cut into large pieces (fat trimmed)
- 3 onions, peeled and quartered
- 2 carrots, peeled and quartered
- 12 large cloves garlic, sliced
- 1 cup dry vermouth or red or white wine* (optional)
- 3 cups chicken broth
- 1 cup chopped celery, with leaves
- 2 bay leaves
- 2 large sprigs rosemary *or* 1 tablespoon dried rosemary, crumbled
- 1 to 2 cups (4 to 8 ounces) shredded JARLSBERG Cheese

*Note: If not using vermouth or wine, increase chicken broth to 4 cups.

Rinse beans; place in large saucepan. Cover with 2 inches water. Bring to a boil over high heat; boil 2 minutes. Remove from heat; cover and let soak 1 hour. Drain beans; discard water. (Or soak beans in cold water overnight; drain and discard water.)

Heat oil in Dutch oven over high heat. Add lamb; cook and stir 10 minutes. Add onions, carrots and garlic; cook and stir 8 minutes, lifting lamb off bottom of pan to let vegetables cook.

Add vermouth, if desired, and cook 3 minutes. Add broth, celery, bay leaves and rosemary; cover and simmer 1½ hours. Add beans and shredded Jarlsberg and continue to simmer 40 minutes to 1 hour until beans are desired firmness. Remove bay leaves and discard before serving.

Makes 8 servings

Garden Fresh Gazpacho

4 large tomatoes (about 2 pounds)
1 large cucumber, peeled and seeded
½ red bell pepper, seeded
½ green bell pepper, seeded
½ red onion
3 cloves garlic
¼ cup *Frank's® RedHot®* Cayenne Pepper Sauce
¼ cup red wine vinegar
3 tablespoons olive oil
2 tablespoons minced fresh basil
1 teaspoon salt
  Additional 2 cups chopped mixed fresh vegetables, such as
  tomatoes, bell peppers, cucumbers and green onions

1. Coarsely chop 4 tomatoes, 1 cucumber, ½ red bell pepper, ½ green bell pepper, ½ red onion and garlic; place in food processor or blender. Add *Frank's RedHot* Sauce, vinegar, oil, basil and salt. Cover; process until very smooth. (Process in batches if necessary.) Transfer soup to large glass serving bowl.

2. Stir in additional chopped vegetables, leaving some for garnish, if desired. Cover; refrigerate 1 hour before serving.

Makes 6 servings (6 cups)

Navy Vegetable Soup with Tortilla Crisps

- 1 cup dried navy beans, sorted and rinsed
- 3 cups water
- 1 teaspoon salt, divided
- 1 pound leeks (about 2), cut into ½-inch pieces
- ¾ pound unpeeled new potatoes
- 2 cups sliced button mushrooms
- 1½ cups thinly sliced carrots
- 6 cups vegetable broth or chicken broth
- 1½ teaspoons dried thyme leaves
- 1 bay leaf
- ½ teaspoon black pepper
- 2 teaspoons olive oil
- 2 corn tortillas (6-inch diameter)
- ¼ teaspoon garlic salt
- 2 medium tomatoes, seeded and chopped

1. Place beans in large saucepan. Add water. Bring to a boil over high heat. Cover and remove from heat. Let stand 30 minutes. Return to a boil over high heat. Reduce heat to low. Cover and simmer 30 minutes. Stir in ½ teaspoon salt. Cover and simmer 1 hour more or until beans are tender; drain.

2. Add leeks, potatoes, mushrooms, carrots, broth, thyme, bay leaf, remaining ½ teaspoon salt and pepper to Dutch oven. Bring to a boil over high heat. Reduce heat to low; cover and simmer 25 minutes. Add bean mixture and cook 5 minutes. Remove bay leaf; discard.

3. Preheat oven to 425°F. Brush oil onto both sides of tortillas. Sprinkle tops of tortillas with garlic salt. Cut into ¼-inch-wide strips. Arrange on baking sheet; bake 10 to 12 minutes or until crisp. Cool.

4. Ladle soup into shallow soup bowls; sprinkle evenly with tomatoes and tortilla crisps. *Makes 8 (1¼-cup) servings*

Navy Vegetable Soup
with Tortilla Crisps

Chicken Tortilla Soup

- 2 large ripe avocados, halved and pitted
- 4 teaspoons TABASCO® brand Green Pepper Sauce, divided
- ½ teaspoon salt or to taste
- 3 (14½-ounce) cans chicken broth
- 3 boneless, skinless chicken breast halves (about 1 pound)
- 2 tablespoons uncooked rice
- 1 large tomato, seeded and chopped
- ½ cup chopped onion
- ¼ cup finely chopped cilantro
  Tortilla chips
- ½ cup (2 ounces) shredded Monterey Jack cheese

Scoop out avocado into medium bowl and mash with fork. Add 1½ teaspoons TABASCO® Green Pepper Sauce and salt; blend gently but thoroughly. Set aside.

Heat chicken broth to boiling in 4-quart saucepan. Add chicken breast halves; reduce heat and cook until chicken is opaque. Remove chicken and cut into bite-size pieces. Add rice and cook about 15 minutes or until tender. Return chicken to saucepan. Just before serving, stir in tomato, onion, cilantro and remaining 2½ teaspoons TABASCO® Green Pepper Sauce.

To serve, break small handful of tortilla chips into bottom of each bowl. Ladle soup over tortilla chips. Top with cheese and 1 rounded tablespoonful avocado mixture. Serve immediately with additional TABASCO® Green Pepper Sauce, if desired.   *Makes 8 servings*

Jamaican Black Bean Stew

2 cups uncooked brown rice
2 pounds sweet potatoes
3 pounds butternut squash
1 large onion, coarsely chopped
1 can (about 14 ounces) vegetable broth
3 cloves garlic, minced
1 tablespoon curry powder
1½ teaspoons ground allspice
½ teaspoon ground red pepper
¼ teaspoon salt
2 cans (15 ounces each) black beans, rinsed and drained
½ cup raisins
3 tablespoons fresh lime juice
1 cup diced tomatoes
1 cup diced peeled cucumber

1. Prepare rice according to package directions. Peel sweet potatoes; cut into ¾-inch chunks to measure 4 cups. Peel squash; remove seeds. Cut flesh into ¾-inch cubes to measure 5 cups.

2. Combine potatoes, squash, onion, broth, garlic, curry powder, allspice, red pepper and salt in Dutch oven. Bring to a boil. Reduce heat to low; simmer, covered, 5 minutes.

3. Add beans and raisins. Simmer 5 minutes or just until sweet potatoes and squash are tender and beans are hot. Remove from heat; stir in lime juice.

4. Serve stew over brown rice and top with tomatoes and cucumber.

Makes 8 servings

Splendid sides

Grilled Asparagus and New Potatoes

1 pound small red potatoes, scrubbed and quartered
¼ cup *French's®* Classic Yellow® Mustard or Napa Valley Style Dijon Mustard
3 tablespoons minced fresh dill *or* 2 teaspoons dried dill weed
3 tablespoons olive oil
3 tablespoons lemon juice
1 tablespoon grated lemon peel
⅛ teaspoon black pepper
1 pound asparagus, washed and trimmed

1. Place potatoes and ¼ cup water in shallow microwavable dish. Cover and microwave on HIGH (100%) 8 minutes or until potatoes are crisp-tender, turning once. Drain.

2. Combine mustard, dill, oil, lemon juice, lemon peel and pepper in small bowl. Brush mixture on potatoes and asparagus. Place vegetables in grilling basket. Grill over medium-high heat 8 minutes or until potatoes and asparagus are fork-tender, turning and basting often with mustard mixture.

Makes 4 servings

Prep Time: 15 minutes
Cook Time: 16 minutes

Mediterranean Grilled Vegetables

4 medium red or Yukon gold potatoes, cooked
3 tablespoons orange juice
2 tablespoons balsamic vinegar
1 clove garlic, minced
½ teaspoon salt
¼ teaspoon black pepper
⅓ cup plus 3 tablespoons olive oil, divided
8 thin slices (4×2 inches) prosciutto or ham (optional)
3 ounces soft goat cheese, cut into 8 pieces (optional)
8 asparagus spears
2 red or yellow bell peppers, cut in half, stemmed and seeded
2 zucchini, cut lengthwise into ¼-inch slices
2 Japanese eggplants, cut lengthwise into ¼-inch slices
1 bulb fennel, cut in half
8 large mushrooms
2 poblano or green bell peppers, cut in half, stemmed and seeded

Cut potatoes into thick slices. Combine juice, vinegar, garlic, salt and black pepper in bowl; whisk in ⅓ cup oil. Set aside. Wrap each slice prosciutto around 1 piece cheese and 1 asparagus spear. Thread cheese bundles onto wooden skewers, piercing asparagus and securing cheese with wooden picks, if necessary. (Soak wooden skewers and picks in hot water 30 minutes to prevent burning.) Brush bundles with remaining 3 tablespoons oil.

Grill bell peppers, skin sides down, over medium KINGSFORD® Briquets 8 minutes until skins are charred. Place in large resealable plastic food storage bag; seal. Let stand 5 minutes; remove skin. Grill remaining vegetables on covered grill over medium briquets 2 to 5 minutes per side until tender. Grill cheese bundles over medium briquets until lightly browned. Arrange vegetables and cheese bundles in 13×9-inch glass dish; drizzle with dressing, turning to coat. Let stand 15 minutes.

Makes 6 to 8 servings

Tip: Japanese eggplants are slender, 5 to 7 inches long and sweeter than larger varieties. They can be purple or purple and white striped.

Fusilli with Fresh Red & Yellow Tomato Sauce

½ cup (1 stick) I CAN'T BELIEVE IT'S NOT BUTTER!® Spread
1 medium onion, chopped
2 cloves garlic, finely chopped (optional)
1½ pounds red and/or yellow cherry tomatoes, halved
⅓ cup chopped fresh basil leaves
1 box (16 ounces) fusilli (long curly pasta) or linguine, cooked and
    drained
Grated Parmesan cheese

In 12-inch nonstick skillet, melt I Can't Believe It's Not Butter!® Spread over medium heat and cook onion, stirring occasionally, 2 minutes or until softened. Stir in garlic and tomatoes and cook, stirring occasionally, 5 minutes or until tomatoes soften but do not lose their shape and sauce thickens slightly. Stir in basil and season, if desired, with salt and ground black pepper.

In large serving bowl, toss sauce with hot fusilli and sprinkle with cheese.

Makes 4 servings

Oven-Roasted Vegetables

1½ pounds assorted cut-up fresh vegetables*
3 tablespoons I CAN'T BELIEVE IT'S NOT BUTTER!® Spread, melted
2 cloves garlic, finely chopped
1 tablespoon chopped fresh oregano leaves *or* 1 teaspoon dried
    oregano leaves, crushed
Salt and ground black pepper to taste

*Use any combination of the following: zucchini; red, green or yellow bell peppers; Spanish or red onions; white or portobello mushrooms; and carrots.

Preheat oven to 450°F. In bottom of broiler pan, without rack, combine all ingredients. Roast 20 minutes or until vegetables are tender, stirring once.

Makes 4 servings

Fusilli with Fresh Red &
Yellow Tomato Sauce

99

Stuffed Portobello Mushrooms

1 box UNCLE BEN'S® Long Grain & Wild Rice Roasted Garlic
2 tablespoons prepared pesto sauce
8 ounces cream cheese, softened
4 large portobello mushrooms
   Salt and black pepper to taste
1 large tomato
4 tablespoons grated Parmesan cheese
4 basil leaves (optional)

COOK: Preheat oven to 400°F. CLEAN: Wash hands. Prepare rice according to package directions. Meanwhile, stir pesto into cream cheese until well blended. Remove stems from mushrooms. Clean mushroom caps well. Place mushrooms, stem side up, on baking sheet. Sprinkle with salt and pepper. Spread one fourth of cream cheese mixture onto each mushroom. Top with ½ cup cooked rice. Slice tomato into 4 thick slices. Place 1 slice on top of rice and sprinkle each mushroom with 1 tablespoon Parmesan cheese. Bake 10 minutes.

SERVE: Serve each mushroom on a separate plate and garnish with basil leaf, if desired.

CHILL: Refrigerate leftovers immediately.   *Makes 4 servings*

Prep Time: none
Cook Time: 30 minutes

Fresh Tip

Always clean mushrooms just before using them. Quickly rinse portobello caps in cool water and dry with paper towels. Do not soak them or they will become soggy.

Pepper and Squash Gratin

    12 ounces russet potatoes, unpeeled
     8 ounces yellow squash, thinly sliced
     8 ounces zucchini, thinly sliced
     2 cups frozen pepper stir-fry blend, thawed
     1 teaspoon dried oregano leaves
    ½ teaspoon salt
       Black pepper to taste
    ½ cup grated Parmesan cheese or shredded reduced-fat sharp
          Cheddar cheese
     1 tablespoon butter or margarine, cut into 8 pieces

1. Preheat oven to 375°F. Coat 12×8-inch glass baking dish with nonstick cooking spray. Pierce potato several times with fork. Microwave at HIGH (100%) 3 minutes; cut into thin slices.

2. Layer half of potatoes, yellow squash, zucchini, pepper stir-fry blend, oregano, salt, black pepper and cheese in prepared baking dish. Repeat layers and top with butter. Cover tightly with foil; bake 25 minutes or until vegetables are just tender. Remove foil and bake 10 minutes or until lightly browned. *Makes 8 servings*

Fresh Tip

This vegetable combination not only tastes delicious but has only 3 grams of fat per serving.

Green Beans with Toasted Pecans

3 tablespoons I CAN'T BELIEVE IT'S NOT BUTTER!® Spread, melted
1 teaspoon sugar
¼ teaspoon garlic powder
    Pinch ground red pepper
    Salt to taste
⅓ cup chopped pecans
1 pound green beans

In small bowl, blend I Can't Believe It's Not Butter!® Spread, sugar, garlic powder, pepper and salt.

In 12-inch nonstick skillet, heat 2 teaspoons garlic mixture over medium-high heat and cook pecans, stirring frequently, 2 minutes or until pecans are golden. Remove pecans and set aside.

In same skillet, heat remaining garlic mixture and stir in green beans. Cook, covered, over medium heat, stirring occasionally, 6 minutes or until green beans are tender. Stir in pecans. *Makes 4 servings*

Broccoli with Tangerine Ginger Sauce

½ cup chopped onion
2 teaspoons chopped crystallized ginger
1 teaspoon margarine
1 carton (8 ounces) low-fat lemon yogurt
    Grated peel of 1 fresh SUNKIST® tangerine
2 SUNKIST® tangerines, peeled, segmented and seeded
1½ pounds broccoli, trimmed *or* 2 packages (10 ounces each) frozen broccoli spears, cooked and drained

In small nonstick skillet over low heat, cook and stir onion and ginger in margarine until onion is very tender. Stir in yogurt, tangerine peel and segments. Cook and stir over low heat until heated through. *Do not boil.* Serve sauce over hot cooked broccoli. Garnish with additional grated tangerine peel, if desired. *Makes 6 servings*

Pepper-Stuffed Artichokes

  4 large artichokes, outer leaves removed
¼ cup lemon juice
  2 teaspoons olive oil
½ cup chopped onion
  2 cloves garlic, minced
½ cup diced red bell pepper
½ cup diced yellow bell pepper
½ cup fresh whole wheat bread crumbs
  2 tablespoons chopped fresh parsley
  2 teaspoons dried oregano leaves
⅛ teaspoon black pepper
  1 can (14½ ounces) no-salt-added peeled tomatoes, undrained
  2 tablespoons freshly grated Parmesan cheese

1. Preheat oven to 350°F. Trim 1 inch off top and stem of each artichoke. Dip artichokes in lemon juice to prevent browning.

2. Bring 5 cups water to boil in large saucepan over high heat. Reduce heat to low; add artichokes and simmer 30 minutes. Drain and cool slightly. Cut in half lengthwise. Scoop out and discard center of artichoke.

3. Heat oil in small nonstick skillet over medium heat. Add onion and garlic; cook and stir 3 to 4 minutes or until onion is tender. Remove from heat; stir in bell peppers, bread crumbs, parsley, oregano and black pepper. Stuff artichokes with bell pepper mixture.

4. Spray 9-inch square baking pan with nonstick cooking spray. Arrange stuffed artichokes in prepared pan. Set aside.

5. Place tomatoes in food processor or blender; process until smooth. Pour over artichokes. Sprinkle with Parmesan cheese. Cover and bake 30 minutes or until lightly browned. *Makes 4 servings*

Marinated Mushrooms, Carrots and Snow Peas

1 cup julienne carrots
1 cup fresh snow peas or sugar snap peas
½ cup water
1 lemon
2 cups small mushrooms
⅔ cup white wine vinegar
2 tablespoons sugar
2 tablespoons chopped fresh parsley
2 tablespoons extra-light olive oil
1 tablespoon chopped fresh thyme
1 clove garlic, minced

1. Combine carrots and peas in 1-quart microwavable dish; add water. Cover and microwave at HIGH (100%) 4 minutes or just until water boils. *Do not drain.*

2. Remove several strips of peel from lemon with vegetable peeler. Finely chop peel to measure 1 teaspoon. Squeeze juice from lemon to measure 2 tablespoons. Combine peel, juice and remaining ingredients in small bowl. Pour over carrot mixture. Cover and refrigerate at least 3 hours.

3. To serve, remove vegetables from marinade with slotted spoon. Place in serving dish; discard marinade.   *Makes 12 servings*

Fresh Tip

When removing strips of peel from the lemon, remove only the yellow portion of the peel but not the white pith underneath. The pith has a bitter flavor.

Savory Skillet Broccoli

1 tablespoon **BERTOLLI®** Olive Oil
6 cups fresh broccoli florets *or* 1 pound green beans, trimmed
1 envelope **LIPTON® RECIPE SECRETS®** Golden Onion Soup Mix*
1½ cups water

*Also terrific with LIPTON® RECIPE SECRETS® Onion-Mushroom Soup Mix.

1. In 12-inch skillet, heat oil over medium-high heat and cook broccoli, stirring occasionally, 2 minutes.

2. Stir in soup mix blended with water. Bring to a boil over high heat.

3. Reduce heat to medium-low and simmer covered 6 minutes or until broccoli is tender. *Makes 4 servings*

Prep Time: 5 minutes
Cook Time: 10 minutes

Ratatouille

1 large onion, thinly sliced into rings
2 zucchini, sliced
2 green bell peppers, cut into strips
1 small eggplant, peeled and cut into ¾-inch cubes
¾ teaspoon **LAWRY'S®** Garlic Powder with Parsley
½ teaspoon (to taste) **LAWRY'S®** Seasoned Salt
½ teaspoon (to taste) **LAWRY'S®** Seasoned Pepper
5 tomatoes, seeded and chopped
1 tablespoon capers (optional)

In 3-quart glass casserole, combine onion, zucchini, green peppers, eggplant and seasonings. Cover with plastic wrap, venting one corner. Microwave on HIGH 8 minutes. Stir in tomatoes; cover and microwave on HIGH 3 to 4 minutes, just until vegetables are tender-crisp and remain colorful. Add capers, if desired. *Makes 6 to 8 servings*

Serving Suggestion: Serve hot or cold with warm pita bread wedges as a relish accompaniment or as a vegetable.

Maple-Glazed Carrots & Shallots

1 package (16 ounces) baby carrots
1 tablespoon margarine or butter
½ cup thinly sliced shallots
2 tablespoons reduced-fat maple-flavored pancake syrup
¼ teaspoon salt
⅛ teaspoon white pepper

1. Place carrots in medium saucepan. Add enough water to cover carrots. Simmer 8 to 10 minutes or until carrots are tender. Drain; set aside.

2. In same saucepan, melt margarine over medium-high heat. Add shallots; cook and stir 3 to 4 minutes or until shallots are tender and beginning to brown. Add drained carrots, syrup, salt and pepper. Cook and stir 1 to 2 minutes or until carrots are coated and heated through.

Makes 4 servings

Roasted Butternut Squash

Nonstick cooking spray
1 pound butternut squash, peeled and cut into 1-inch cubes
   (about 4 cups)
2 medium onions, coarsely chopped
8 ounces carrots, peeled and cut into ½-inch diagonal slices
   (about 2 cups)
1 tablespoon dark brown sugar
¼ teaspoon salt
Black pepper to taste
1 tablespoon butter or margarine, melted

Preheat oven to 400°F. Line large baking sheet with foil; coat with cooking spray. Arrange vegetables in single layer on foil; coat lightly with cooking spray. Sprinkle vegetables with brown sugar, salt and pepper.

Bake 30 minutes. Stir gently; bake 10 to 15 minutes longer or until vegetables are tender. Remove from oven; drizzle with butter and toss to coat.

Makes 5 (1-cup) servings

Swiss-Style Vegetables

¾ cup cubed unpeeled red potato
2 cups broccoli florets
1 cup cauliflower florets
2 teaspoons margarine
1 cup sliced mushrooms
1 tablespoon all-purpose flour
1 cup fat-free half-and-half
½ cup reduced-fat grated Swiss cheese
¼ teaspoon salt
¼ teaspoon black pepper
¼ teaspoon hot pepper sauce (optional)
⅛ teaspoon ground nutmeg
¼ cup grated Parmesan cheese

1. Place potato in medium saucepan; cover with cold water. Bring water to a boil. Reduce heat; cover and simmer 10 minutes. Add broccoli and cauliflower; cover and cook about 5 minutes or until all vegetables are tender. Drain; remove vegetables to medium bowl. Set aside.

2. Melt margarine in same pan over medium-low heat. Add mushrooms. Cook and stir 2 minutes. Stir in flour; cook 1 minute. Slowly stir in half-and-half; cook and stir until mixture thickens. Remove from heat. Add Swiss cheese, stirring until melted. Stir in salt, pepper, pepper sauce, if desired, and nutmeg.

3. Preheat broiler. Spray small shallow casserole with nonstick cooking spray.

4. Arrange vegetables in single layer in prepared casserole. Spoon sauce mixture over vegetables; sprinkle with Parmesan cheese.

5. Place casserole under broiler until cheese is melted and brown, about 1 minute.   *Makes 6 servings*

Creamy Roasted Garlic Mashed Potatoes

**3 medium all-purpose potatoes, peeled and cubed (about
1½ pounds)**
3 medium cloves garlic, unpeeled
¼ cup I CAN'T BELIEVE IT'S NOT BUTTER!® Spread
¼ cup milk, heated to boiling
½ teaspoon salt
Pinch ground black pepper

In 2-quart saucepan, add potatoes and fill with water to cover. Bring to a
boil over high heat. Reduce heat to low and simmer uncovered 20 minutes
or until potatoes are very tender.

Meanwhile, heat 8-inch nonstick skillet over medium-low heat. Add garlic
and cook, turning occasionally, 15 minutes or until garlic is tender and skin
is golden. Remove garlic; peel, then finely chop.

Drain potatoes and return to saucepan. Add garlic, I Can't Believe It's Not
Butter! Spread, milk, salt and pepper; mash until smooth.

Makes 4 servings

Fresh Tip

*All-purpose potatoes are long and oval in shape with
thin light brown skins. They average about 8 ounces
each. They can be boiled, baked or fried.*

Brussels Sprouts in Mustard Sauce

1½ pounds fresh brussels sprouts*
1 tablespoon butter or margarine
⅓ cup chopped shallots or onion
⅓ cup half-and-half
1 tablespoon plus 1½ teaspoons tarragon Dijon mustard** or
Dusseldorf mustard
¼ teaspoon salt
⅛ teaspoon black pepper or ground nutmeg
1½ tablespoons grated Parmesan cheese (optional)

*Or, substitute 2 (10-ounce) packages frozen brussels sprouts for fresh brussels sprouts. Cook according to package directions; drain and rinse as directed. Proceed with step 2.

**Or, substitute 1 tablespoon plus 1½ teaspoons Dijon mustard and ½ teaspoon dried tarragon leaves, crushed, for tarragon Dijon mustard.

1. Cut stem from each brussels sprout and pull off outer bruised leaves. Cut an "X" deep into stem end of each brussels sprout. Cut large brussels sprouts lengthwise into halves. Bring 2 quarts salted water to a boil in large saucepan. Add brussels sprouts; return to a boil. Boil uncovered 7 to 10 minutes or until almost tender when pierced with fork. Drain. Rinse under cold water; drain thoroughly.

2. Melt butter in same saucepan over medium heat. Add shallots; cook 3 minutes, stirring occasionally. Add half-and-half, mustard, salt and pepper. Simmer 1 minute or until thickened. Add brussels sprouts; heat about 1 minute or until heated through, tossing gently with sauce. Sprinkle with cheese, if desired. *Makes 6 to 8 servings*

Cheese-Stuffed Pattypans

4 pattypan squash (about 3 inches in diameter)
4 tablespoons butter or margarine
2 ribs celery, diced
½ cup chopped onion
½ cup water
1 cup dry herb-seasoned stuffing mix
1 cup (4 ounces) shredded sharp Cheddar cheese

1. Preheat oven to 350°F. To prepare pattypans, wash and slice off top, above scalloped edge; discard tops. Scoop out seeds and discard.

2. Place squash shells in large skillet. Pour ¼ inch of water into skillet; cover. Bring to a boil over high heat; reduce heat to medium-low. Simmer 5 minutes. Transfer squash, cut side up, to greased 8×8-inch baking dish with slotted spoon.

3. Heat butter in large skillet over medium-high heat until bubbly. Cook and stir celery and onion in butter until tender. Add water, then stuffing mix. Stir to absorb water. Stir in cheese. Divide mixture among squash.

4. Bake 20 to 30 minutes or until squash is fork-tender and stuffing is lightly browned. Garnish as desired. Serve immediately.

Makes 4 side-dish servings

Fresh Tip

The small size (3 to 4 inches in diameter) of these squash makes them perfect for individual servings. They are most commonly found in the summer months.

Light Lemon Cauliflower

4 tablespoons chopped fresh parsley, divided
½ teaspoon grated lemon peel
6 cups (about 1½ pounds) cauliflower florets
1 tablespoon reduced-fat margarine
3 cloves garlic, minced
2 tablespoons fresh lemon juice
¼ cup shredded Parmesan cheese

1. Place 1 tablespoon parsley, lemon peel and about 1 inch of water in large saucepan. Place cauliflower in steamer basket and place in saucepan. Bring water to a boil over medium heat. Cover and steam 14 to 16 minutes or until cauliflower is crisp-tender. Remove to large bowl; keep warm. Reserve ½ cup hot liquid.

2. Heat margarine in small saucepan over medium heat. Add garlic; cook and stir 2 to 3 minutes or until soft. Stir in lemon juice and reserved liquid.

3. Spoon lemon mixture over cauliflower. Sprinkle with remaining 3 tablespoons parsley and cheese before serving. Garnish with lemon slices, if desired. *Makes 6 servings*

Summer Vegetable Medley

2 medium carrots
2 medium yellow squash
2 medium zucchini
1 tablespoon olive oil
1 tablespoon butter
2 teaspoons dried Italian seasoning
Fresh basil (optional)

Slice vegetables into $3 \times \frac{1}{8}$-inch strips. Heat oil and butter in large skillet over medium-high heat. Add carrots; cook and stir 1 minute. Add yellow squash, zucchini and Italian seasoning; cook and stir until vegetables are crisp-tender. Place vegetables in serving bowl. Garnish with fresh basil, if desired. *Makes 4 to 6 servings*

Blooming salads

Ginger Shrimp Salad

- **1 package (10 ounces) DOLE® French Salad Blend or Italian Salad Blend**
- **6 ounces cooked shelled and deveined medium shrimp or cooked tiny shrimp**
- **1 can (11 ounces) DOLE® Mandarin Oranges, drained**
- **1 medium DOLE® Red, Yellow or Green Bell Pepper, cut into 2-inch strips**
- **⅓ cup fat free or reduced fat mayonnaise**
- **⅓ cup DOLE® Pineapple Juice**
- **2 teaspoons finely chopped fresh ginger *or* ¼ teaspoon ground ginger**

• Toss salad blend, shrimp, mandarin oranges and bell pepper in large serving bowl.

• Stir mayonnaise, juice and ginger in small bowl. Add to salad; toss to evenly coat.   *Makes 3 servings*

Prep Time: 20 minutes

California Crab Salad

1 packet (.4 ounce) **HIDDEN VALLEY®** The Original Ranch® Buttermilk
    Recipe Salad Dressing Mix
1 cup buttermilk
1 cup mayonnaise
1 tablespoon grated fresh ginger
1 teaspoon prepared horseradish
2 cups cooked white rice, chilled
4 lettuce leaves
8 ounces cooked crabmeat, chilled
1 large ripe avocado, thinly sliced
½ medium cucumber, thinly sliced

In medium bowl, whisk together salad dressing mix, buttermilk and mayonnaise. Whisk in ginger and horseradish. Cover and refrigerate 30 minutes. To serve, arrange ½ cup rice on top of each lettuce leaf. Top with 2 tablespoons of the dressing. Arrange one quarter of the crabmeat, avocado and cucumber on top of each rice mound. Serve with remaining dressing. Garnish with cherry tomatoes and lime wedges, if desired.

Makes 4 servings

Italian Tortellini Salad

2 cups broccoli florets
½ cup sliced carrot
8 ounces tortellini, cooked and cooled
1 cup (6 ounces) **CURE 81®** ham cut into strips
1 cup sliced green bell pepper
1 cup sliced red bell pepper
½ cup sliced red onion
½ cup creamy Italian salad dressing

Cook broccoli and carrot in boiling water 2 to 3 minutes or until crisp-tender; drain. Cool. In large bowl, combine broccoli, carrot, cooked tortellini, ham, bell peppers and onion. Toss with dressing.

Garden Pasta Salad

1½ cups snow peas
1½ cups sliced carrots
1½ cups cauliflower florets
   8 ounces BARILLA® Campanelle, cooked according to package
      directions
½ cup honey dijon salad dressing

1. Cook snow peas, carrots and cauliflower in boiling water 3 minutes; drain.

2. Combine cooked campanelle and vegetables in large bowl.

3. Just before serving, add salad dressing; toss lightly.

Makes 6 to 8 servings

Tip: Serve with additional dressing on the side.

Spinach Salad with Apricots and Peanuts

6 tablespoons apricot preserves
3 tablespoons apple cider vinegar
½ cup peanut oil
1 pound spinach, cleaned, patted dry and torn into bite-sized pieces
1 (15-ounce) can mandarin oranges, drained
¾ cup dry roasted Texas peanuts, coarsely chopped

Combine preserves and vinegar in blender; process until smooth, stopping once to scrape down sides. With blender on high speed, gradually add peanut oil in a slow, steady stream. Blend until thickened.

Combine spinach, half of the oranges, half of the peanuts and dressing in a large salad bowl; toss gently. Top with remaining oranges and sprinkle with remaining peanuts. Serve immediately.

Makes 8 servings

Favorite recipe from *Texas Peanut Producers Board*

Vegetable Potato Salad

1 envelope LIPTON® RECIPE SECRETS® Vegetable Soup Mix
1 cup HELLMANN'S® or BEST FOODS® Mayonnaise
2 teaspoons white vinegar
2 pounds red or all-purpose potatoes, cooked and cut into chunks
¼ cup finely chopped red onion (optional)

1. In large bowl, combine soup mix, mayonnaise and vinegar.

2. Add potatoes and onion; toss well. Chill 2 hours.   *Makes 6 servings*

Prep Time: 20 minutes
Chill Time: 2 hours

Sweet-Sour Turnip Green Salad

2 cups shredded stemmed washed turnip greens
2 cups washed mixed salad greens
1 cup sliced plum tomatoes or quartered cherry tomatoes
½ cup shredded carrot
⅓ cup sliced green onions
8 tablespoons water, divided
2 teaspoons all-purpose flour
1 tablespoon packed brown sugar
½ teaspoon celery seeds
Dash black pepper
1 tablespoon white wine vinegar

Combine turnip greens, salad greens, tomatoes and carrot in salad bowl; set aside. Combine green onions and 2 tablespoons water in small saucepan. Bring to a boil over high heat. Reduce heat to medium. Cook, covered, 2 to 3 minutes or until onions are tender.

Mix remaining 6 tablespoons water and flour in small bowl until smooth. Stir into green onions in saucepan. Add brown sugar, celery seeds and pepper; cook and stir until mixture boils and thickens. Cook and stir 1 minute more. Stir in vinegar. Pour hot dressing over salad; toss to coat. Serve immediately.   *Makes 4 servings*

Winter Pear and Stilton Salad

⅓ cup extra-virgin olive oil
1 tablespoon plus 1½ teaspoons sherry wine vinegar or white wine
　　vinegar
4 teaspoons honey
1 tablespoon Dijon mustard
¼ teaspoon salt
2 ripe Bosc, Bartlett or Anjou pears
　　Lemon juice
5 cups assorted gourmet mixed salad greens (such as oakleaf,
　　frisee, watercress, radicchio, arugula or escarole), torn into
　　bite-size pieces
2 cups torn Boston or Bibb lettuce leaves
1½ cups (6 ounces) Stilton or Gorgonzola cheese, crumbled
　　Black pepper

1. Place oil, vinegar, honey, mustard and salt in small bowl. Whisk together until well blended. Cover and refrigerate up to 2 days.

2. Cut pears into quarters; remove stem and core. Cut each quarter into ½-inch pieces. To help prevent discoloration, brush pear pieces with lemon juice, if desired.

3. Combine all salad greens in large bowl. Add pears, cheese and dressing. Toss lightly to coat; sprinkle with pepper.　　　　*Makes 6 to 8 servings*

Sun Country Chicken Salad

- 1 large cantaloupe
- 2 cups cubed cooked chicken
- 1 cup cucumber chunks
- 1 cup green grapes
- ½ cup chopped green onions
- 2 tablespoons chopped fresh parsley
- 1 cup plain nonfat yogurt
- 3 tablespoons prepared chutney
- 1 tablespoon lemon juice
- ¼ teaspoon grated lemon peel
- ¼ cup whole blanched California Almonds, toasted*
- 1 large bunch watercress

*To toast, spread almonds in a single layer on baking sheet. Toast at 350°F, 5 to 8 minutes, stirring occasionally, until lightly browned. Cool.

Cut cantaloupe into 12 wedges, removing seeds and peel. Combine chicken, cucumber, grapes, onions and parsley in medium bowl. Blend together yogurt, chutney, lemon juice and lemon peel in small bowl. Toss lightly with chicken mixture. Fold in almonds. Arrange watercress on 4 salad plates. Place 3 wedges of cantaloupe on each plate. Spoon chicken salad mixture over cantaloupe. *Makes 4 servings*

Favorite recipe from *Almond Board of California*

Fresh Tip

When selecting watercress, avoid wilted, bruised or yellowing leaves as these are signs of inferior quality.

Thai Beef Salad

¾ cup mayonnaise
¾ cup unsweetened coconut milk
1 packet (1 ounce) **HIDDEN VALLEY®** The Original Ranch® Salad
　　Dressing & Seasoning Mix
2 tablespoons lime juice
1 pound thinly sliced roast beef
1 English cucumber, thinly sliced
1 cup sliced bamboo shoots (optional)
¼ cup cilantro leaves
¼ cup coarsely chopped peanuts

Combine mayonnaise, coconut milk, salad dressing & seasoning mix and lime juice in a small bowl; chill 30 minutes. Arrange beef, cucumber, bamboo shoots, if desired, and cilantro on a large platter. Pour dressing in a thin stream over salad. Sprinkle with peanuts. *Makes 4 servings*

Chilean Nectarine, Grape and Raspberry Salad

4 ripe Chilean nectarines
1 small bunch red seedless Chilean grapes
1 small bunch green seedless Chilean grapes
2 medium zucchini
½ cup olive oil
2 tablespoons raspberry vinegar
　Salt and black pepper
　Leaf lettuce leaves
1 cup Chilean raspberries

Halve nectarines and cut into wedges. Pull grapes from stems; there should be about 1 cup of red and 1 cup of green. Cut zucchini into sticks. Whisk together olive oil and raspberry vinegar in small bowl; season to taste with salt and pepper. Line 4 salad plates with lettuce leaves and arrange nectarine slices, grapes, zucchini sticks and raspberries decoratively on top. Drizzle with dressing. *Makes 4 servings*

Favorite recipe from **Chilean Fresh Fruit Association**

Warm Salmon Salad

Chive Vinaigrette (page 137)
2 cups water
¼ cup chopped onion
2 tablespoons red wine vinegar
¼ teaspoon black pepper
1¼ pounds small unpeeled red potatoes
1 pound salmon steaks
6 cups torn washed mixed salad greens
2 medium tomatoes, cut into wedges
16 kalamata olives,* sliced

*Kalamata olives are imported from Greece and can be found at many large supermarkets and gourmet food specialty shops.

1. Prepare Chive Vinaigrette; refrigerate.

2. Combine water, onion, vinegar and pepper in large saucepan; bring to a boil over medium-high heat. Add potatoes. Cover; simmer 10 minutes or until fork-tender. Transfer potatoes to cutting board using slotted spoon; cool slightly. Reserve water.

3. Cut potatoes into thick slices; place in medium bowl. Toss potatoes with ⅓ cup Chive Vinaigrette; set aside.

4. Rinse salmon and pat dry with paper towels. To poach fish, add fish to reserved water and simmer gently 4 to 5 minutes or until fish is opaque and flakes easily when tested with fork. *Do not boil.*

5. Carefully remove fish from saucepan with slotted spatula to cutting board. Let stand 5 minutes. Remove and discard skin and bones from fish; cut fish into 1-inch pieces.

6. Place salad greens onto 4 plates. Arrange fish, potatoes, tomatoes and olives on top. Drizzle with remaining Chive Vinaigrette.

Makes 4 servings

Chive Vinaigrette

⅓ cup vegetable oil
¼ cup red wine vinegar
2 tablespoons finely chopped fresh chives
2 tablespoons finely chopped fresh parsley
⅛ teaspoon salt
⅛ teaspoon white pepper

Combine oil, vinegar, chives, parsley, salt and pepper in jar with tight-fitting lid; shake well to combine. *Makes about ⅔ cup*

Warm Salmon Salad

Smoked Turkey, Vegetable and Rotini Salad

1 can (15½ ounces) artichoke hearts, rinsed, drained and halved
8 ounces rotini pasta, cooked and cooled to room temperature
8 ounces brussels sprouts, halved and cooked crisp-tender
8 ounces asparagus, cut into 1½-inch pieces and cooked
    crisp-tender
8 ounces smoked turkey breast, cut into ¾-inch cubes
1 red bell pepper, sliced
  Mustard Seed Vinaigrette (recipe follows)
  Salt and black pepper
  Salad greens
1 tablespoon pine nuts or slivered almonds, toasted

Combine artichokes, pasta, brussels sprouts, asparagus, turkey and bell pepper in large bowl; drizzle with Mustard Seed Vinaigrette and toss. Season to taste with salt and black pepper. Serve on salad greens; sprinkle with pine nuts. *Makes 4 main-dish servings*

Mustard Seed Vinaigrette

3 tablespoons olive oil
2 tablespoons water
1 clove garlic, minced
½ teaspoon Dijon mustard
¼ teaspoon mustard seeds, crushed

Combine all ingredients in jar with tight-fitting lid; refrigerate until serving time. Shake well before using. *Makes about ½ cup*

Smoked Turkey, Vegetable
and Rotini Salad

139

Citrus Salad with Bibb Lettuce, Watercress and Balsamic Dressing

1 medium pink Florida grapefruit, peeled, white pith removed and
    sectioned
2 large Florida oranges, peeled, white pith removed and sectioned
2 tangerines, peeled and sectioned
1 bunch watercress, rinsed and patted dry
3 tablespoons Florida orange juice
1 tablespoon balsamic vinegar
¼ teaspoon salt
1 tablespoon canola or vegetable oil
1 large head Bibb lettuce, separated, rinsed and patted dry
    Peel of 1 Florida orange, cut into julienne strips

1. Combine grapefruit, oranges, tangerines and watercress in medium bowl. Combine orange juice, vinegar and salt in small bowl. Add oil; whisk dressing until combined. Pour over fruit and watercress; gently toss to combine.

2. Line 4 serving plates with lettuce. Divide fruit mixture among plates. Garnish each with orange peel.   *Makes 4 servings*

Favorite recipe from *Florida Department of Citrus*

Blooming salads

Colorful Grape, Pepper and Pasta Salad

8 ounces dry thin spaghetti, cooked
Mustard Vinaigrette (recipe follows)
1 cup California seedless grapes
½ cup thinly sliced red or yellow bell pepper
2 tablespoons minced celery
2 tablespoons green onion
1 tablespoon chopped fresh tarragon*
Salt and pepper to taste
¼ cup walnuts, quartered**
Fresh tarragon sprigs (optional)

*You can substitute ½ teaspoon dried tarragon, crushed, for fresh tarragon.

**Walnuts can be omitted; substitute 1 tablespoon walnut oil for 1 tablespoon olive oil in vinaigrette.

Combine cooked spaghetti and 3 tablespoons Mustard Vinaigrette; toss to coat. Cool. Add remaining ingredients including remaining vinaigrette; mix well. Serve in lettuce-lined bowl; garnish with tarragon, if desired.

Makes 4 servings

Mustard Vinaigrette: Combine 3 tablespoons white wine vinegar, 2 tablespoons olive oil, 2 tablespoons Dijon mustard, 1 clove minced garlic, ½ teaspoon sugar and ⅛ teaspoon pepper; mix well

Favorite recipe from *California Table Grape Commission*

Gazpacho Salad

1½ cups peeled and coarsely chopped tomatoes*
 1 cup peeled, seeded, diced cucumber
 ¾ cup chopped onion
 ½ cup chopped red bell pepper
 ½ cup fresh or frozen corn kernels, cooked and drained
 1 tablespoon lime juice
 1 tablespoon red wine vinegar
 2 teaspoons water
 1 teaspoon minced fresh garlic
 1 teaspoon extra-virgin olive oil
 ¼ teaspoon salt
 ¼ teaspoon black pepper
   Pinch ground red pepper
 1 medium head romaine lettuce, torn into bite-size pieces
 1 cup peeled, diced jicama
 ½ cup fresh cilantro sprigs

*To peel tomatoes easily, blanch in boiling water 30 seconds; immediately transfer to bowl of cold water, then peel.

1. Combine tomatoes, cucumber, onion, bell pepper and corn in large bowl. Combine lime juice, vinegar, water, garlic, oil, salt, black pepper and ground red pepper in small bowl; whisk until well blended. Pour over tomato mixture; toss well. Cover and refrigerate several hours to allow flavors to blend.

2. Toss together lettuce, jicama and cilantro in another large bowl. Divide lettuce mixture evenly among 6 plates. Place ⅔ cup chilled tomato mixture on top of lettuce. *Makes 6 servings*

Mandarin Turkey Salad with Buttermilk-Herb Dressing

Buttermilk-Herb Dressing (recipe follows)
1 can (about 14 ounces) fat-free, reduced-sodium chicken broth
1¼ pounds turkey tenderloins, cut in half lengthwise
½ teaspoon dried basil leaves
½ pound (about 8 cups) mesclun salad greens, washed and dried
2 pounds (about 10 cups) raw cut-up vegetables, such as broccoli
   florets, red or yellow bell peppers, carrots and red onion
1 can (11 ounces) mandarin orange segments, drained

1. Prepare Buttermilk-Herb Dressing. Cover and refrigerate.

2. Place broth in medium saucepan; bring to a boil over high heat. Add turkey and basil. Return to a boil; reduce heat. Simmer, covered, 12 to 14 minutes or until turkey is no longer pink.

3. Remove turkey from broth. When cool enough to handle, shred turkey into strips.

4. Arrange salad greens on individual plates. Divide turkey evenly over salad greens. Arrange vegetables and orange segments around turkey; drizzle each serving with 2 tablespoons Buttermilk-Herb Dressing.

Makes 6 servings

Buttermilk-Herb Dressing

½ cup plus 1 tablespoon nonfat buttermilk
3 tablespoons raspberry-flavored vinegar
1 tablespoon chopped fresh basil leaves
1½ teaspoons snipped fresh chives
¼ teaspoon minced garlic

Place all ingredients in small bowl; stir to combine. *Makes about ¾ cup*

FREE PREVIEW ISSUE

BEST RECIPES™ Every recipe **15g carbs or less** per serving

All-New
LOW-CARB *Lifestyle*

Recipes for breakfasts, sides, main dishes, and desserts

Low-Carb, High-Flavor Recipes!

Yes! Send my FREE preview issue of LOW-CARB LIFESTYLE Magazine today and start my subscription. If I like what I see, I'll get three more issues for only $9.95—that's a 38% savings off the cover price! If I'm not delighted, I'll just write "cancel" on the invoice and owe nothing. I'll keep the FREE issue no matter what.

Name

Address

City/State/ZIP

Above rate for U.S. subscriptions only. Canada and foreign, add $4, payable in U.S. funds. Canada and foreign, payment must be included with order. Please allow 4-6 weeks for delivery of free preview issue.

No risk. No obligation.
Just mail this card today! S69DGA

BUSINESS REPLY MAIL

FIRST-CLASS MAIL PERMIT NO. 24 MT. MORRIS, IL

POSTAGE WILL BE PAID BY ADDRESSEE

**LOW-CARB LIFESTYLE
PO BOX 512
MT MORRIS IL 61054-7912**

Hidden Valley® Chopstick Chicken Salad

1 packet (1 ounce) **HIDDEN VALLEY®** The Original Ranch® Salad
    Dressing & Seasoning Mix
1 cup milk
1 cup mayonnaise
2 tablespoons soy sauce
8 cups torn lettuce
2 cups shredded cooked chicken
1 cup chopped green onions
1 cup chopped water chestnuts
1 cup toasted sliced almonds (optional)

In a bowl, combine salad dressing & seasoning mix with milk and mayonnaise. Mix well. Cover and refrigerate. Chill 30 minutes to thicken. Stir in soy sauce. Toss with lettuce, chicken, onions and water chestnuts; top with almonds, if desired. *Makes 4 to 6 servings*

Note: To prepare Lower Fat Hidden Valley® The Original Ranch® Salad Dressing & Seasoning Mix, substitute low-fat milk and light mayonnaise for regular milk and mayonnaise.

Napa Valley Chicken Salad

2 cups diced cooked chicken
1 cup seedless red grapes, halved
1 cup diced celery
½ cup chopped toasted pecans
¼ cup thinly sliced green onions
½ cup **HIDDEN VALLEY®** The Original Ranch® Dressing
1 teaspoon Dijon mustard

Combine chicken, grapes, celery, pecans and onions in a medium bowl. Stir together dressing and mustard; toss with salad. Cover and refrigerate for 2 hours. *Makes 4 servings*

Raspberry Mango Salad

    2 cups arugula
    1 cup torn Bibb or Boston lettuce
    ½ cup watercress, stems removed
    1 cup diced mango
    ¾ cup fresh raspberries
    ¼ cup (1½ ounces) crumbled blue cheese
    1 tablespoon olive oil
    1 tablespoon water
    1 tablespoon raspberry vinegar
    ⅛ teaspoon salt
    ⅛ teaspoon black pepper

1. Combine arugula, lettuce, watercress, mango, raspberries and cheese in medium bowl.

2. Shake remaining ingredients in small jar. Pour over salad; toss to coat. Serve immediately. *Makes 4 servings*

Easy Chef's Salad

    1 package (16 ounces) DOLE® Classic Iceberg Salad (8 cups)
    1½ cups DOLE® Broccoli cut into florets
    1 large tomato, cut into thin wedges
    4 ounces deli-sliced smoked turkey or chicken, cut into ½-inch
        strips
    ¾ cup cubed low fat Cheddar, Monterey Jack or mozzarella cheese
    ¼ cup feta or goat cheese
    ¾ cup fat free or light ranch salad dressing

• Toss together salad, broccoli, tomato, turkey and cheeses in large serving bowl.

• Pour dressing over salad; toss to evenly coat. *Makes 4 servings*

Prep Time: 15 minutes

Flank Steak Salad with Wine-Mustard Dressing

1 flank steak (about 1½ pounds) *or* 3½ cups thinly sliced cooked
    roast beef
2 tablespoons white wine vinegar
1 tablespoon Dijon mustard
½ teaspoon LAWRY'S® Seasoned Pepper
6 tablespoons vegetable oil
1 pound small red potatoes, cooked and sliced
½ pound fresh green beans, steamed until tender-crisp
1 jar (6 ounces) marinated artichoke hearts, drained
¼ pound mushrooms, sliced
5 green onions including tops, sliced

Grill or broil steak 10 to 12 minutes or until desired doneness, turning
halfway through grilling time. In small bowl, combine vinegar, mustard and
Seasoned Pepper; mix well with wire whisk. Slowly add oil, beating
constantly. Thinly slice steak on the diagonal across the grain. Cut each
slice into 2-inch strips. Place in large salad bowl; add dressing and toss
gently. Add remaining ingredients and toss. Serve at room temperature.

Makes 6 to 8 servings

Serving Suggestion: Arrange bed of lettuce on individual plates and serve
steak and vegetable mixture on top.

Hint: For extra flavor, marinate steak in Lawry's® Seasoned Marinade or
Dijon & Honey Marinade with Lemon Juice.

Fresh Green Salad with Orange Segments and Fat-Free Honey Dressing

¼ cup water
¼ cup white wine vinegar with tarragon or red wine vinegar
¼ cup honey
2 heads butter lettuce
1 head radicchio, leaves separated
2 oranges, peeled and separated into segments

Combine water, vinegar and honey in small jar; cover and shake to mix ingredients. Arrange lettuce and radicchio on 6 salad plates. Divide orange segments among salad plates; drizzle each with dressing.

Makes 6 servings

Favorite recipe from **National Honey Board**

Sesame Shrimp Avocado Salad

2 teaspoons sesame seeds
2 tablespoons I CAN'T BELIEVE IT'S NOT BUTTER!® Spread
1 pound shrimp, peeled and deveined
6 cups assorted mixed greens
1 large avocado, peeled and sliced
1 large orange, peeled and sectioned
6 radishes, sliced (optional)
    Your favorite WISH-BONE® Vinaigrette Dressing

In 12-inch nonstick skillet, toast sesame seeds over medium-high heat until golden, about 2 minutes. Remove sesame seeds and set aside.

In same skillet, melt I Can't Believe It's Not Butter! Spread over medium-high heat and cook shrimp, sprinkled, if desired, with salt and ground black pepper, until shrimp turn pink, about 4 minutes, turning once.

To serve, arrange mixed greens on serving platter. Top with avocado, orange, radishes and shrimp. Sprinkle with toasted sesame seeds. Just before serving, drizzle with dressing.

Makes 4 servings

Fresh Green Salad with Orange
Segments and Fat-Free Honey Dressing

153

Divine
desserts

Speedy Pineapple-Lime Sorbet

1 ripe pineapple, peeled and cut into cubes (about 4 cups)
⅓ cup frozen limeade concentrate, thawed
1 to 2 tablespoons fresh lime juice
1 teaspoon grated lime peel

1. Arrange pineapple in single layer on large jelly-roll pan; freeze at least 1 hour or until very firm. Transfer pineapple to resealable plastic freezer food storage bag; freeze up to 1 month.

2. Combine frozen pineapple, limeade, lime juice and lime peel in food processor; process until smooth and fluffy. If pineapple doesn't become smooth and fluffy, let stand 30 minutes to soften slightly; then repeat processing. Serve immediately. *Makes 8 servings*

Note: This dessert is best if served immediately; but it may be made ahead, stored in the freezer, then softened several minutes before serving.

Very Strawberry Pie

1 container (8 ounces) strawberry-flavored soft cream cheese
4 containers (4 ounces each) refrigerated vanilla pudding snacks
2 tablespoons strawberry-flavored sundae topping
1 (6-ounce) ready-to-use chocolate or shortbread crust
1 pint strawberries

1. Place cream cheese in small bowl; beat 30 seconds at low speed of electric mixer. Add pudding and topping; beat 1 minute or until blended.

2. Pour mixture into crust. Refrigerate 10 minutes.

3. While pie is chilling, wash and hull strawberries. Cut into halves or slices. Arrange on top of pie.   *Makes 6 servings*

Serving Suggestion: For a special touch, drizzle top of pie with strawberry-flavored or chocolate ice cream topping just before serving.

Prep Time: 17 minutes

Hot Rum-Glazed Bananas over Ice Cream

2 tablespoons butter
2 tablespoons dark brown sugar
2 tablespoons honey
¾ teaspoon TABASCO® brand Pepper Sauce
4 bananas, cut into 1-inch slices
3 tablespoons dark rum
4 (¼-cup) scoops vanilla ice cream
Chocolate syrup

Combine butter, brown sugar, honey and TABASCO® Sauce in large skillet; cook over medium-high heat until mixture sizzles. Add bananas; toss gently until each slice is coated. Increase heat to high; add rum and cook 20 seconds or until mixture has syrupy consistency and bananas are glazed.

Scoop ice cream into bowls; spoon warm bananas on top. Drizzle with chocolate syrup and serve immediately.   *Makes 4 servings*

Upside-Down Pear Tart

½ cup sugar
2 tablespoons butter or margarine
2 teaspoons grated lemon peel
5 medium (2½ to 3 pounds) firm Northwest winter pears, peeled,
     cored and cut into eight slices
1 tablespoon lemon juice
   Pastry for 9-inch single crust pie

Heat sugar over medium heat in heavy 10-inch skillet with oven-safe handle until syrupy and light brown in color. Remove from heat and add butter and lemon peel; stir until butter melts. Arrange pears in two layers over hot sugar mixture in skillet. Fill open spaces with pear slices; sprinkle with lemon juice. Roll pastry to 10-inch round and place over pears. Bake at 425°F 25 to 30 minutes or until pastry is golden brown. Cool in pan 30 minutes. If there seems to be too much sauce in pan, pour excess sauce into 1-pint container and reserve to serve over tart. Invert tart onto shallow serving dish. Serve warm with vanilla yogurt.   *Makes 6 to 8 servings*

Favorite recipe from *Pear Bureau Northwest*

Peach Ice Cream

7 fresh California peaches, peeled, halved and pitted
2 cups 2% low-fat milk
1 envelope unflavored gelatin
1 cup plain low-fat yogurt
½ cup sugar
1 tablespoon vanilla

Chop enough peaches to measure 1 cup. Add remaining peaches to food processor; process to measure 2½ cups purée. Combine milk and gelatin in medium saucepan. Heat, stirring, until gelatin dissolves; remove from heat. Add chopped peaches, peach purée, yogurt, sugar and vanilla; mix well. Prepare in ice cream maker according to manufacturer's directions. Transfer to containers and freeze until firm.   *Makes 7 servings*

Favorite recipe from *California Tree Fruit Agreement*

Nectarine Blueberry Crisp

3 cups cubed unpeeled nectarines
2 cups fresh blueberries
2 tablespoons granulated sugar
1 tablespoon cornstarch
½ teaspoon ground cinnamon
¼ cup all-purpose flour
¼ cup uncooked quick oats
¼ cup chopped walnuts
3 tablespoons dark brown sugar
2 tablespoons toasted wheat germ
2 tablespoons reduced-fat margarine, melted
¼ teaspoon ground nutmeg

1. Preheat oven to 400°F. Spray bottom and side of 9-inch round or square baking pan with nonstick cooking spray. Combine nectarines, blueberries, granulated sugar, cornstarch and cinnamon in medium bowl. Transfer to prepared pan; bake 15 minutes.

2. Meanwhile, combine remaining ingredients in small bowl, stirring with fork until crumbly. Remove fruit mixture from oven; sprinkle with topping. Return to oven; bake 20 minutes longer or until fruit is bubbly and topping is lightly browned. Serve warm.   *Makes 6 servings*

All-American Pineapple & Fruit Trifle

1 DOLE® Fresh Pineapple
1 cup frozen sliced peaches, thawed
1 cup frozen strawberries, thawed, sliced
1 cup frozen raspberries, thawed
1 (10-inch) angel food cake
1 package (4-serving size) vanilla flavor sugar free instant pudding
    and pie filling mix
⅓ cup cream sherry
½ cup frozen whipped topping, thawed

Divine desserts

- Twist crown from pineapple. Cut pineapple in half lengthwise. Refrigerate one half for another use, such as fruit salad. Cut fruit from shell. Cut fruit into thin wedges. Reserve 3 wedges for garnish; combine remaining pineapple with peaches and berries.

- Cut cake in half. Freeze one half for another use. Tear remaining cake into chunks.

- Prepare pudding mix according to package directions.

- In 2-quart glass serving bowl, arrange half of cake chunks; sprinkle with half of sherry. Top with half each fruit mixture and pudding. Repeat layers. Cover; chill 1 hour or overnight.

- Just before serving, garnish with whipped topping and reserved pineapple wedges. *Makes 8 to 10 servings*

Peanutty Cranberry Bars

½ cup (1 stick) butter or margarine, softened
½ cup granulated sugar
¼ cup packed light brown sugar
 1 cup all-purpose flour
 1 cup quick-cooking rolled oats
¼ teaspoon baking soda
¼ teaspoon salt
 1 cup REESE'S® Peanut Butter Chips
1½ cups fresh or frozen whole cranberries
⅔ cup light corn syrup
½ cup water
 1 teaspoon vanilla extract

1. Heat oven to 350°F. Grease 8-inch square baking pan.

2. Beat butter, granulated sugar and brown sugar in medium bowl until fluffy. Stir together flour, oats, baking soda and salt; gradually add to butter mixture, mixing until mixture is consistency of coarse crumbs. Stir in peanut butter chips.

3. Reserve 1½ cups mixture for crumb topping. Firmly press remaining mixture evenly into prepared pan. Bake 15 minutes or until set. Meanwhile, in medium saucepan, combine cranberries, corn syrup and water. Cook over medium heat, stirring occasionally, until mixture boils. Reduce heat; simmer 15 minutes, stirring occasionally. Remove from heat. Stir in vanilla. Spread evenly over baked layer. Sprinkle reserved 1½ cups crumbs evenly over top.

4. Return to oven. Bake 15 to 20 minutes or until set. Cool completely in pan on wire rack. Cut into bars.   *Makes about 16 bars*

Brandied Fruit

2 large ripe mangos, papayas or peaches
2 to 3 large ripe plums, halved and pitted
24 sweet cherries, halved and pitted
6 tablespoons sugar
¼ cup brandy
2 tablespoons chopped crystallized ginger
1 tablespoon fresh lemon juice
2 teaspoons cornstarch
1 tablespoon orange- or cherry-flavored liqueur (optional)
Angel food cake (optional)

1. Spray grillproof 9-inch square baking pan or pie plate with nonstick cooking spray; set aside. Peel mangos; slice pulp from pit and cut into ½-inch-wide slices. Place in prepared baking pan. Cut each plum half into 4 wedges; add to pan. Stir in cherries.

2. Combine sugar, brandy, ginger, lemon juice and cornstarch in small bowl until cornstarch dissolves; pour over fruit. Cover tightly with foil.

3. Place on grid and grill on covered grill over low to medium coals 20 to 30 minutes or until juices simmer and fruit is tender; stir in liqueur, if desired. Spoon over angel food cake, if desired, or serve in small bowls. Garnish as desired. *Makes 6 servings*

Tip: Firm fruits hold up best on the grill. Consider stirring in fresh berries after removing the grilled fruit from the heat and covering for a few minutes to warm through.

Summertime Fruit Medley

2 large ripe peaches, peeled and sliced
2 large ripe nectarines, sliced
1 large mango, peeled and cut into 1-inch chunks
1 cup blueberries
2 cups orange juice
¼ cup amaretto *or* ½ teaspoon almond extract
2 tablespoons sugar

1. Combine peaches, nectarines, mango and blueberries in large bowl.

2. Whisk orange juice, amaretto and sugar in small bowl until sugar is dissolved. Pour over fruit mixture; toss. Marinate 1 hour at room temperature, gently stirring occasionally. Garnish with mint, if desired.

Makes 8 servings

Apple Crisp

10 Golden Delicious apples (about 5 pounds), peeled, cored and sliced (about 12 cups)
1 cup firmly packed brown sugar, divided
2 teaspoons ground cinnamon
¾ cup all-purpose flour
½ cup (1 stick) IMPERIAL® Spread
¾ cup uncooked quick or old-fashioned oats

Preheat oven to 375°F.

In large bowl, combine apples, ½ cup sugar and cinnamon. Turn into 13×9-inch baking pan or 3-quart shallow casserole; set aside.

In medium bowl, combine flour and remaining ½ cup sugar. With pastry blender or 2 knives, cut in spread until mixture is size of coarse crumbs. Stir in oats. With hands, gently squeeze mixture to form crumbs; sprinkle over apple mixture.

Bake, uncovered, 1 hour or until apples are tender and topping is golden. Serve warm or at room temperature and, if desired, with vanilla ice cream or frozen yogurt.

Makes 8 servings

Pineapple Daiquiri Sundae

  1 pineapple, cored, peeled and cut into ½-inch chunks
  ½ cup sugar
  ½ cup dark rum
  3 tablespoons lime juice
     Zest of 2 limes, cut in long strands
  1 tablespoon cornstarch or arrowroot

Slow Cooker Directions

Place all ingredients in slow cooker; mix well. Cover and cook on HIGH 3 to 4 hours. Serve hot over ice cream, pound cake or shortcakes. Garnish with fresh raspberries and mint leaves, if desired.

Makes 4 to 6 servings

Tip: Substitute 1 can (20 ounces) crushed pineapple, drained, for the fresh pineapple. Cook on HIGH 3 hours.

Fresh Nectarine-Pineapple Cobbler

1½ cups DOLE® Fresh Pineapple, cut into chunks
  3 cups sliced ripe DOLE® Fresh Nectarines or Peaches
  ½ cup sugar
  2 tablespoons all-purpose flour
  ½ teaspoon ground cinnamon
  1 cup buttermilk baking mix
  ½ cup low-fat milk

• Combine pineapple, nectarines, sugar, flour and cinnamon in 8×8-inch glass baking dish; spread fruit evenly in dish.

• Stir together baking mix and milk in small bowl until just combined. Pour over fruit.

• Bake at 400°F 40 to 45 minutes or until fruit is tender and crust is browned.

Makes 8 servings

Prep Time: 20 minutes
Bake Time: 45 minutes

Divine desserts

Plum Streusel

Plum Filling
- ½ cup firmly packed light brown sugar
- 3 tablespoons cornstarch
- ½ teaspoon ground nutmeg
- 2½ pounds ripe plums, pitted and sliced ½ inch thick

Streusel
- 1 cup all-purpose flour
- ½ Butter Flavor CRISCO® Stick or ½ cup Butter Flavor CRISCO® all-vegetable shortening
- ½ cup firmly packed light brown sugar
- 1 teaspoon ground cinnamon
- 1 teaspoon vanilla
- ¼ teaspoon salt

1. Heat oven to 350°F. Spray 3-quart shallow baking dish with CRISCO® No-Stick Cooking Spray; set aside.

2. For filling, combine brown sugar, cornstarch and nutmeg in large bowl; mix well. Add plums and stir gently to coat evenly. Place in prepared pan.

3. For streusel, combine flour, shortening, ½ cup brown sugar, cinnamon, vanilla and salt in large bowl. Mix with fork until mixture is combined and just crumbly. *Do not overmix.* Sprinkle over fruit mixture.

4. Bake at 350°F for 45 minutes or until streusel top is crisp. Cool about 10 minutes; serve warm with whipped cream or ice cream.

Makes 6 to 8 servings

Tip: Streusel is the German word for "sprinkle" and that is exactly how you're going to add the topping. This easy dessert is perfect for summer holiday entertaining.

White & Chocolate Covered Strawberries

1⅔ cups (10-ounce package) HERSHEY'S Premier White Chips
2 tablespoons shortening (do not use butter, margarine, spread or oil)
4 cups (2 pints) fresh strawberries, rinsed, patted dry and chilled
1 cup HERSHEY'S Semi-Sweet Chocolate Chips

1. Cover tray with wax paper.

2. Place white chips and 1 tablespoon shortening in medium microwave-safe bowl. Microwave at HIGH (100%) 1 minute; stir until chips are melted and mixture is smooth. If necessary, microwave at HIGH an additional 30 seconds at a time, just until smooth when stirred.

3. Holding by top, dip ⅔ of each strawberry into white chip mixture; shake gently to remove excess. Place on prepared tray; refrigerate until coating is firm, at least 30 minutes.

4. Repeat microwave procedure with chocolate chips in clean microwave-safe bowl. Dip lower ⅓ of each berry into chocolate mixture. Refrigerate until firm. Cover; refrigerate leftover strawberries.

Makes 2 to 3 dozen berries

California Plum Sorbet

12 fresh California plums, halved, pitted and sliced
1 cup orange juice
3 tablespoons sugar
1 tablespoon grated orange peel

1. Add plums, orange juice, sugar and orange peel to food processor or blender; process until smooth. Pour into loaf pan; freeze about 4 hours.

2. Process again 30 minutes before serving. Freeze until ready to serve.

Makes 6 servings

Favorite recipe from *California Tree Fruit Agreement*

Sundae Shortcakes

    1 cup sugar
    ⅓ cup thawed frozen orange juice concentrate
    ⅓ cup water
    3 tablespoons butter
    1 can (about 17 ounces) buttermilk biscuits
    1 pint frozen vanilla or fruit-flavored yogurt or vanilla ice cream
    3 cups fresh or frozen blackberries, thawed
    Frozen whipped topping, thawed

1. Combine sugar, orange juice concentrate, water and butter in small saucepan. Bring to a boil over medium-high heat, stirring constantly until sugar is melted. Boil gently, uncovered, 5 minutes.

2. Prepare biscuits according to package directions. Pierce 4 biscuits all over with skewer. Spoon ¼ of sugar mixture over 4 biscuits. Reserve remaining biscuits for another use. Let stand 1 minute.

3. Split biscuits; place bottom halves on serving plates. Spoon yogurt evenly over bottoms; top with blackberries. Drizzle with remaining sugar mixture; top with biscuit tops.   *Makes 4 servings*

Serving Suggestion: Serve with frozen whipped topping.

Prep & Cook Time: 30 minutes

Carrot Layer Cake

Cake
- **1 package DUNCAN HINES® Moist Deluxe® Classic Yellow Cake Mix**
- **3 cups grated carrots**
- **1 cup finely chopped nuts**
- **4 eggs**
- **½ cup vegetable oil**
- **2 teaspoons ground cinnamon**

Cream Cheese Frosting
- **1 package (8 ounces) cream cheese, softened**
- **¼ cup butter or margarine, softened**
- **2 teaspoons vanilla extract**
- **4 cups confectioners' sugar**

1. Preheat oven to 350°F. Grease and flour two 8- or 9-inch round baking pans.

2. For cake, combine cake mix, carrots, nuts, eggs, oil and cinnamon in large bowl. Beat at low speed with electric mixer until moistened. Beat at medium speed for 2 minutes. Pour into prepared pans. Bake at 350°F for 35 to 40 minutes or until toothpick inserted in centers comes out clean. Cool completely.

3. For cream cheese frosting, place cream cheese, butter and vanilla extract in large bowl. Beat at low speed until smooth and creamy. Add confectioners' sugar gradually, beating until smooth. Add more sugar to thicken, or milk or water to thin frosting, as needed. Fill and frost cooled cake. Garnish with whole pecans. *Makes 12 to 16 servings*

Chocolate Raspberry Cheesecake

2 (3-ounce) packages cream cheese, softened
1 (14-ounce) can sweetened condensed milk
1 egg
3 tablespoons lemon juice
1 teaspoon vanilla
1 cup fresh or frozen raspberries
1 (6-ounce) READY CRUST® Chocolate Pie Crust
Chocolate Glaze (recipe follows)

1. Preheat oven to 350°F. Beat cream cheese in medium bowl with electric mixer at medium speed until fluffy. Gradually beat in sweetened condensed milk until smooth. Add egg, lemon juice and vanilla; mix well. Arrange raspberries on bottom of crust. Slowly pour cream cheese mixture over raspberries.

2. Bake 30 to 35 minutes or until center is almost set. Cool on wire rack.

3. Prepare Chocolate Glaze; spread over cheesecake. Refrigerate 3 hours. Garnish as desired. Refrigerate leftovers. *Makes 8 servings*

Chocolate Glaze: Melt 2 (1-ounce) squares semisweet baking chocolate with ¼ cup whipping cream in small saucepan over low heat. Cook and stir until thickened and smooth. Remove from heat.

Prep Time: 15 minutes
Chill Time: 3 hours

The Wild Berry Sundae

Blueberries, raspberries, blackberries and/or strawberries, rinsed
   and patted dry
Scoops of vanilla ice cream
HERSHEY'S Chocolate Shoppe™ Hot Fudge Topping
REDDI-WIP® Whipped Topping

• Alternate layers of berries with ice cream and HERSHEY'S Chocolate
Shoppe Hot Fudge topping in sundae dish.

• Top with REDDI-WIP Whipped Topping.   *Makes 1 sundae*

Spiced Pear with Vanilla Ice Cream

2 teaspoons butter, softened
1 tablespoon brown sugar
¼ teaspoon pumpkin pie spice
1 large Bosc pear, halved lengthwise and cored
   Lemon juice
2 scoops vanilla ice cream

1. Preheat toaster oven or oven to 450°F. Coat center of 18×12-inch
heavy-duty foil sheet with butter.

2. Combine sugar and pumpkin pie spice in small bowl. Sprinkle sugar
mixture over butter. Sprinkle cut sides of pear halves with lemon juice.
Place pear halves, cut side down, side by side on sugar mixture.

3. Double fold sides and ends of foil to seal foil packet, leaving headspace
for heat circulation. Place packet on toaster oven tray or baking sheet.

4. Bake 40 minutes or until pear halves are tender. Remove from oven. Let
stand 15 minutes.

5. Open packet and transfer pear halves to serving plates. Spoon sauce
over pears. Serve with ice cream.   *Makes 2 servings*

Sautéed Mangoes & Peaches with Peanut Brittle Topping

2 tablespoons butter
2 large ripe peaches, cut into wedges
1 medium ripe mango, peeled, pitted and sliced
1 tablespoon brown sugar
4 scoops vanilla ice cream
½ cup peanut brittle, crushed

1. Melt butter over medium-high heat in large nonstick skillet Add peach and mango slices; sprinkle with brown sugar. Cook and stir gently 3 to 4 minutes or until heated through and fruit begins to soften.

2. Divide fruit equally among 4 individual dessert bowls. Top each with 1 scoop ice cream and peanut brittle. *Makes 4 servings*

Note: Purchased mango slices in light syrup packed in jars may be substituted for fresh mango slices. Look for them in the refrigerated section of the supermarket produce section. Drain well before using.

Prep & Cook Time: 17 minutes

Easy Orange Ice Cream

2 cups heavy cream or whipping cream
1 cup sugar
⅓ cup fresh squeezed SUNKIST® lemon juice
   Grated peel of 1 SUNKIST® orange
⅓ cup fresh squeezed SUNKIST® orange juice

In large bowl, combine cream and sugar; stir to dissolve sugar. Add lemon juice; continue stirring. (Mixture will thicken slightly.) Stir in orange peel and juice. Pour into shallow pan; freeze until firm, about 4 hours. Serve in dessert dishes. *Makes 6 servings*

Sautéed Mangoes & Peaches with
Peanut Brittle Topping   181

Lemon Cheesecake

Crust
- **35 vanilla wafers**
- **¾ cup slivered almonds, toasted**
- **⅓ cup sugar**
- **¼ cup butter, melted**

Filling
- **3 packages (8 ounces each) cream cheese, softened**
- **¾ cup sugar**
- **4 eggs**
- **⅓ cup whipping cream**
- **¼ cup lemon juice**
- **1 tablespoon grated lemon peel**
- **1 teaspoon vanilla**

Topping
- **1 pint strawberries**
- **2 tablespoons sugar**

1. Preheat oven to 375°F. For crust, combine wafers, almonds and ⅓ cup sugar in food processor; process until fine crumbs are formed. Combine crumb mixture with melted butter in medium bowl. Press mixture evenly on bottom and 1 inch up side of 9-inch springform pan. Set aside.

2. For filling, beat cream cheese and ¾ cup sugar in large bowl on high speed of electric mixer 2 to 3 minutes or until fluffy. Add eggs one at a time, beating briefly after each addition. Add whipping cream, lemon juice, lemon peel and vanilla; beat just until blended. Pour into prepared crust. Place springform pan on baking sheet. Bake 45 to 55 minutes or until set. Cool 10 minutes on wire rack; loosen rim of pan but do not remove. Cool completely. Cover and refrigerate at least 10 hours or overnight.

3. For topping, hull and slice strawberries. Combine with sugar in medium bowl. Let stand 15 minutes. Serve over cheesecake.   *Makes 16 servings*

Apple Golden Raisin Cheesecake Bars

1½ cups rolled oats
¾ cup all-purpose flour
½ cup firmly packed light brown sugar
¾ cup plus 2 tablespoons granulated sugar, divided
¾ Butter Flavor CRISCO® Stick or ¾ cup Butter Flavor CRISCO®
   all-vegetable shortening
2 (8-ounce) packages cream cheese, softened
2 eggs
1 teaspoon vanilla
1 cup chopped Granny Smith apples
½ cup golden raisins
1 teaspoon almond extract
½ teaspoon ground cinnamon
¼ teaspoon ground nutmeg
¼ teaspoon ground allspice

1. Heat oven to 350°F.

2. Combine oats, flour, brown sugar and ¼ cup granulated sugar in large bowl; mix well. Cut in shortening with fork until crumbs form. Reserve 1 cup mixture.

3. Spray 13×9-inch baking pan with CRISCO® No-Stick Cooking Spray. Press remaining mixture onto bottom of prepared pan. Bake at 350°F for 12 to 15 minutes or until mixture is set. *Do not brown.* Place on cooling rack.

4. Combine cream cheese, eggs, ½ cup granulated sugar and vanilla in large bowl. Beat at medium speed with electric mixer until well blended. Spread evenly over crust.

5. Combine apples and raisins in medium bowl. Add almond extract; stir. Add 2 tablespoons sugar, cinnamon, nutmeg and allspice; mix well. Top cream cheese mixture evenly with apple mixture; sprinkle reserved oat mixture evenly over top. Bake at 350°F for 20 to 25 minutes or until top is golden. Place on cooling rack; cool completely. Cut into bars.

Makes 18 bars

 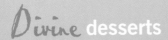

Apple Golden Raisin Cheesecake Bars 185

Berry Cobbler Cake

2 cups (1 pint) fresh berries (blueberries, blackberries, and/or
    raspberries)
1 package (1-layer size) yellow cake mix
1 teaspoon ground cinnamon
1 egg
1 cup water, divided
¼ cup sugar
1 tablespoon cornstarch
    Ice cream (optional)

1. Preheat oven to 375°F.

2. Place berries in 9×9-inch baking pan; set aside.

3. Combine cake mix and cinnamon in large bowl. Add egg and ¼ cup
water; stir until blended. Spoon over berries.

4. Combine sugar and cornstarch in small bowl. Stir in remaining ¾ cup
water until sugar mixture dissolves; pour over cake batter and berry
mixture.

5. Bake 40 to 45 minutes or until lightly browned. Serve warm or cool
with ice cream, if desired.   *Makes 6 servings*

Mango-Peach Frozen Yogurt

2 medium (8 ounces each) ripe mangoes, peeled and cubed
2 cups peach low-fat yogurt
½ cup honey

In blender or food processor container, process mango cubes until smooth.
Add yogurt and honey; process until well combined. Transfer mixture to
ice cream maker; freeze according to manufacturer's directions.

                                               Makes 6 servings

Favorite recipe from **National Honey Board**

Fresh Nectarine Pie with Strawberry Topping

Pie Crust (recipe follows)
1½ pounds nectarines, pitted and cut into ½-inch-thick slices
½ cup sugar, divided
1 pint strawberries, hulled
1 tablespoon lemon juice
1 tablespoon cornstarch

Preheat oven to 425°F. Prepare Pie Crust. Reserve 6 to 8 nectarine slices for garnish. Chop remaining nectarines; place into pie crust. Sprinkle evenly with 2 tablespoons sugar. Bake 30 minutes or until crust is browned and fruit is easily pierced with sharp knife. Let cool, uncovered, on wire rack 30 minutes or until room temperature.

Meanwhile, place strawberries in food processor; process until strawberries are puréed. Press purée through strainer, discarding seeds and pulp. Pour liquid into 1-cup measure. Add lemon juice and enough water to equal 1 cup liquid.

Combine remaining 6 tablespoons sugar with cornstarch in small saucepan. Gradually blend in strawberry mixture until sugar and cornstarch are dissolved. Bring to a boil over medium heat. Cook and stir 5 minutes or until mixture boils and thickens. Remove from heat; let cool 15 minutes. Spoon mixture over pie, spreading to cover nectarines. Let cool completely.

Refrigerate at least 2 hours or up to 8 hours before serving. Cover with plastic wrap after 1 hour in refrigerator. *Makes 8 servings*

Pie Crust

1¼ cups all-purpose flour
¼ teaspoon baking powder
Dash salt
¼ cup canola or vegetable oil
3 tablespoons fat-free (skim) milk, divided

Combine flour, baking powder and salt in medium bowl. Add oil and 2 tablespoons milk; mix well. Add enough remaining milk to hold mixture together. Shape dough into a ball.

Flatten dough to 1-inch thickness on 12-inch square of waxed paper; cover with second square of waxed paper. Roll out gently into 12-inch round. Mend any tears or ragged edges by pressing together with fingers. *Do not moisten.* Remove 1 layer of waxed paper. Place dough, paper side up, in 9-inch pie pan. Carefully peel off remaining paper. Press pastry gently into pan and flute edge.   *Makes one (12-inch) crust*

Fresh Nectarine Pie with Strawberry Topping

Bountiful brunches

Breakfast Burritos with Tomato-Basil Topping

  1 large tomato, diced
  2 teaspoons finely chopped basil *or* ½ teaspoon dried basil leaves
  1 medium potato, peeled and shredded (about 1 cup)
¼ cup chopped onion
  2 teaspoons FLEISCHMANN'S® Original Margarine
  1 cup EGG BEATERS® Healthy Real Egg Product
⅛ teaspoon ground black pepper
  4 (8-inch) flour tortillas, warmed
⅓ cup shredded reduced-fat Cheddar cheese

In small bowl, combine tomato and basil; set aside.

In large nonstick skillet, over medium heat, sauté potato and onion in margarine until tender. Pour Egg Beaters® into skillet; sprinkle with pepper. Cook, stirring occasionally until mixture is set.

Divide egg mixture evenly between tortillas; top with cheese. Fold tortillas over egg mixture. Top with tomato mixture.   *Makes 4 servings*

Prep Time: 15 minutes
Cook Time: 25 minutes

Blueberry-Cheese Pancakes

    2 cups all-purpose flour
    2 teaspoons baking powder
    ¼ teaspoon baking soda
    ¼ teaspoon salt
    2 tablespoons sugar
    2 tablespoons wheat germ
 1½ cups milk
    1 cup cottage cheese, pressed through a sieve
    1 egg, lightly beaten
    ¼ cup vegetable oil
    1 cup fresh blueberries

1. Sift flour, baking powder, baking soda and salt into medium bowl. Stir in sugar and wheat germ; set aside.

2. Combine milk, cottage cheese, egg and oil in small bowl.

3. Pour liquid ingredients, all at once, into dry ingredients; stir until moistened. Add additional milk if batter is too thick; it should pour easily from spoon. Gently stir in blueberries.

4. Preheat griddle or large skillet over medium heat; grease lightly. Pour about ½ cup batter onto hot griddle for each pancake. Cook until tops of pancakes are bubbly and appear dry; turn and cook until lightly browned, about 2 minutes.   *Makes about 10 pancakes*

Note: You can keep pancakes warm until ready to serve by placing them on a plate or baking dish in a 200°F oven. Layer paper towels between pancakes to absorb steam and keep them from getting soggy.

Cranberry Streusel Coffee Cake

          1 egg
      ½ cup plus 3 tablespoons sugar, divided
      ½ cup milk
        1 tablespoon vegetable oil
        1 tablespoon orange juice
        1 teaspoon grated orange peel
      ¼ teaspoon almond extract
    1 ½ cups all-purpose flour, divided
        2 teaspoons baking powder
      ½ teaspoon salt
        8 ounces (2 cups) fresh cranberries
        2 tablespoons butter

1. Preheat oven to 375°F.

2. Beat egg in large bowl. Add ½ cup sugar, milk, oil, orange juice, orange peel and almond extract; mix thoroughly. Combine 1 cup flour, baking powder and salt; add to egg mixture and stir, being careful not to overmix. Pour into 8×8×2-inch pan sprayed with nonstick cooking spray.

3. Chop cranberries in blender or food processor; spoon over batter. Mix remaining ½ cup flour and remaining 3 tablespoons sugar. Cut in butter with pastry blender or 2 knives until mixture resembles coarse crumbs; sprinkle over cranberries.

4. Bake 25 to 30 minutes. Serve warm.   *Makes 9 servings*

California Croissants

1 teaspoon vinegar
4 eggs
2 croissants, halved and toasted
4 slices tomato
½ avocado, sliced crosswise
8 slices crisp-cooked bacon
Mornay Sauce (recipe follows)
Chopped chives and sprouts for garnish

1. Fill wide saucepan or deep skillet with about 1½ inches water. Add vinegar.* Bring to a simmer. Break 1 egg into shallow cup or saucer. Gently slide egg into simmering water. Repeat with remaining eggs.

2. Cook eggs 3 to 4 minutes or until set. Carefully remove eggs with slotted spoon; drain on paper towels.

3. Place croissant half on each plate. Layer tomato, avocado and bacon on croissant. Top with poached eggs. Divide Mornay Sauce equally among croissants. Garnish with chives and sprouts. *Makes 4 servings*

*Adding vinegar to the water helps keep the egg white intact while poaching.

Mornay Sauce

2 tablespoons butter or margarine
2 tablespoons all-purpose flour
1½ cups milk
¼ cup (1 ounce) shredded Cheddar cheese
2 tablespoons grated Parmesan cheese
½ teaspoon Dijon-style mustard
¼ teaspoon salt
⅛ teaspoon white pepper

1. Melt butter in medium saucepan over medium heat. Add flour; stir until bubbly.

2. Gradually stir in milk. Cook, stirring constantly, until mixture comes to a boil. Continue cooking until thickened.

3. Stir in cheeses, mustard, salt and pepper. Remove from heat and continue stirring until cheese melts. *Makes about 1¾ cups*

Puff Pancake with Summer Berries

Summer Berries (recipe follows)
4 tablespoons butter or margarine, divided
2 eggs
½ cup all-purpose flour
½ cup milk
1 tablespoon sugar
¼ teaspoon salt

1. Prepare Summer Berries; set aside. Preheat oven to 425°F. Place 2 tablespoons butter in ovenproof skillet. Place skillet in oven 3 minutes or until butter is bubbly. Swirl pan to coat bottom and side.

2. Beat eggs in medium bowl with electric mixer at high speed. Add flour, milk, remaining 2 tablespoons butter, sugar and salt; beat until smooth.

3. Pour batter into prepared skillet. Bake 15 minutes.

4. *Reduce oven temperature to 350°F.* Continue baking 10 to 15 minutes or until pancake is puffed and golden brown.

5. Serve pancake in skillet with Summer Berries.   *Makes 6 servings*

Summer Berries

2 cups blueberries
1 cup sliced strawberries
1 cup raspberries
Sugar to taste
Whipping cream (optional)

Combine blueberries, strawberries and raspberries in medium bowl. Gently toss with sugar. Let stand 5 minutes. Top with cream, if desired.

Apple and Brie Omelet

2 large Golden Delicious apples
2 tablespoons butter or margarine, divided
½ teaspoon ground nutmeg
4 ounces Brie cheese
8 large eggs, lightly beaten
2 green onions, thinly sliced

1. Place large serving platter in oven; preheat oven to 200°F. Peel, core and slice apples; place in microwavable container. Top with 1 tablespoon butter and nutmeg. Cover and microwave at HIGH (100%) 3 minutes. Set aside. While apples cook, trim rind from cheese; thinly slice cheese.

2. Melt 1½ teaspoons butter in medium nonstick skillet over medium heat; rotate skillet to coat bottom. Place eggs in medium bowl and whisk until blended. Pour half of eggs into skillet. Let cook, without stirring, 1 to 2 minutes, or until set on bottom. With rubber spatula, lift sides of omelet and slightly tilt pan to allow uncooked portion of egg flow underneath. Cover pan and cook 2 to 3 minutes, until eggs are set but still moist on top. Remove platter from oven and slide omelet into center. Spread apples evenly over entire omelet, reserving a few slices for garnish, if desired. Evenly space cheese slices over apples. Sprinkle with onion, reserving some for garnish. Return platter to oven.

3. Cook remaining beaten eggs in remaining 1½ teaspoons butter as directed above. When cooked, slide spatula around edges to be certain omelet is loose. Carefully place second omelet over apple mixture. Top with reserved apple and onion slices. Cut into wedges to serve.

Makes 4 servings

Breakfast Kabobs

2 cups plain yogurt
4 tablespoons honey
1 (12-ounce) package **BOB EVANS®** Original or Maple Links
1 medium cantaloupe melon, peeled, seeded and cut into 1-inch cubes
1 medium honeydew melon, peeled, seeded and cut into 1-inch cubes
1 small bunch green seedless grapes
1 small bunch red seedless grapes
2 medium red apples, cored and cut into 1-inch cubes
1 pint strawberries, hulled and cut into halves

Combine yogurt and honey in small bowl; refrigerate until ready to serve. Cook sausage in medium skillet over medium heat until browned. Drain on paper towels; cut each link in half. Alternately place sausage and fruit on wooden skewers (about 7). Serve kabobs with yogurt sauce for dipping.

Makes about 7 kabobs

Fresh Tip

The fruit can be prepared ahead and refrigerated until ready to assemble kabobs with warm sausage. Brush apples with lemon or orange juice to prevent discoloration.

Mexican Omelet Roll-Ups with Avocado Sauce

8 eggs
2 tablespoons milk
1 tablespoon margarine or butter
1½ cups (6 ounces) shredded Monterey Jack cheese
1 large tomato, seeded and chopped
¼ cup chopped fresh cilantro
8 (7-inch) corn tortillas
1½ cups salsa
2 medium avocados, chopped
¼ cup reduced-fat sour cream
2 tablespoons diced green chilies
1 tablespoon fresh lemon juice
1 teaspoon hot pepper sauce
¼ teaspoon salt

1. Preheat oven to 350°F. Spray 13×9-inch baking dish with nonstick cooking spray.

2. Whisk eggs and milk in medium bowl until blended. Melt margarine in large skillet over medium heat; add egg mixture to skillet. Cook and stir 5 minutes or until eggs are set, but still soft. Remove from heat. Stir in cheese, tomato and cilantro.

3. Spoon about ⅓ cup egg mixture evenly down center of each tortilla. Roll up tortillas and place, seam side down, in prepared dish. Pour salsa evenly over tortillas.

4. Cover tightly with foil and bake 20 minutes or until heated through.

5. Meanwhile, process avocados, sour cream, chilies, lemon juice, pepper sauce and salt in food processor or blender until smooth. Serve tortillas with avocado sauce. *Makes 8 servings*

Tip: To reduce amount of fat in recipe, omit avocado sauce and serve with additional salsa and nonfat sour cream.

Mexican Omelet Roll-Up
with Avocado Sauce

Raspberry-Applesauce Coffee Cake

1½ cups fresh raspberries
¼ cup water
7 tablespoons sugar, divided
2 tablespoons cornstarch
½ teaspoon ground nutmeg, divided
1¾ cups all-purpose flour, divided
3 tablespoons margarine
1 tablespoon finely chopped walnuts
1½ teaspoons baking powder
½ teaspoon baking soda
⅛ teaspoon ground cloves
1 cup unsweetened applesauce
2 egg whites

1. Preheat oven to 350°F. Spray 8-inch square baking pan with nonstick cooking spray.

2. Combine raspberries and water in small saucepan; bring to a boil over high heat. Reduce heat to medium. Combine 2 tablespoons sugar, cornstarch and ¼ teaspoon nutmeg in small bowl. Stir into raspberry mixture. Cook and stir until mixture boils and thickens. Cook and stir 2 minutes more.

3. Combine ¾ cup flour and remaining 5 tablespoons sugar in medium bowl. Cut in margarine with pastry blender until mixture resembles coarse meal. Set aside ½ cup mixture for topping; stir walnuts into remaining crumb mixture.

4. Add remaining 1 cup flour, baking powder, baking soda, remaining ¼ teaspoon nutmeg and cloves to walnut mixture; mix well. Stir in applesauce and egg whites; beat until well combined. Spread half of batter into prepared pan. Spread raspberry mixture over batter. Drop remaining batter in small mounds on top. Sprinkle with reserved topping.

5. Bake 40 to 45 minutes or until edges start to pull away from sides of pan. Serve warm or cool. *Makes 9 servings*

Eggs Benedict

Mock Hollandaise Sauce (recipe follows)
6 cups water
4 eggs, divided
2 English muffins, halved
Fresh spinach leaves, washed and drained
8 ounces sliced lean Canadian bacon
4 tomato slices, cut ¼ inch thick
Paprika

1. Prepare Mock Hollandaise Sauce. Set aside.

2. Bring water to a boil in large saucepan over high heat. Reduce heat and simmer. Carefully break 1 egg into small dish and slide egg into water. Repeat with remaining 3 eggs. Simmer, uncovered, about 5 minutes or until yolks are just set.

3. Meanwhile, toast muffin halves; place on serving plates. Top each muffin half with spinach leaves, 2 ounces Canadian bacon, 1 tomato slice and 1 egg. Spoon 3 tablespoons Mock Hollandaise Sauce over egg; sprinkle with paprika. Serve with fresh fruit, if desired.   *Makes 4 servings*

Mock Hollandaise Sauce

4 ounces fat-free cream cheese
3 tablespoons plain nonfat yogurt
1 tablespoon lemon juice
1 teaspoon Dijon mustard

Process all ingredients in food processor or blender until smooth. Heat in small saucepan over medium-high heat until hot.

Makes about ¾ cup sauce

Cranberry Oat Bread

¾ cup honey
⅓ cup vegetable oil
2 eggs
½ cup milk
2½ cups all-purpose flour
1 cup quick-cooking rolled oats
1 teaspoon baking soda
1 teaspoon baking powder
½ teaspoon salt
½ teaspoon ground cinnamon
2 cups fresh or frozen cranberries
1 cup chopped nuts

Combine honey, oil, eggs and milk in large bowl; mix well. Combine flour, oats, baking soda, baking powder, salt and cinnamon in medium bowl; mix well. Stir into honey mixture. Fold in cranberries and nuts. Spoon into two 8½×4½×2½-inch greased and floured loaf pans.

Bake in preheated 350°F oven 40 to 45 minutes or until wooden toothpick inserted near centers comes out clean. Cool in pans on wire racks 15 minutes. Remove from pans; cool completely on wire racks.

Makes 2 loaves

Favorite recipe from **National Honey Board**

Fresh Tip

Fresh cranberries are readily available in the fall. Buy extra bags of them before the holidays when prices are low, then freeze them for use throughout the year.

Apple Brunch Strata

½ **pound sausage, casing removed**
4 **cups cubed French bread**
2 **cups diced peeled Michigan Apples**
¼ **cup sliced green onions**
⅓ **cup sliced black olives**
1½ **cups (6 ounces) shredded sharp Cheddar cheese**
2 **cups reduced-fat milk**
8 **eggs**
2 **teaspoons spicy brown mustard**
½ **teaspoon salt**
¼ **teaspoon black pepper**
Paprika

1. Brown sausage in skillet over medium-high heat. Drain on paper towels; set aside.

2. Spray 13×9×2-inch baking dish with nonstick cooking spray. Layer half of bread cubes in bottom of dish. Crumble sausage over bread. Top with Michigan Apples, green onions, olives and cheese. Place remaining bread on top.

3. Mix milk, eggs, mustard, salt and pepper in medium bowl; pour over bread. Cover with foil and refrigerate 4 hours or overnight.

4. Preheat oven to 350°F. Bake, covered, 45 minutes. Remove foil and bake 15 minutes or until center is set. Let stand 15 minutes before serving. Sprinkle with paprika, if desired. *Makes 8 servings*

Tip: Suggested Michigan Apple varieties to use include Empire, Gala, Golden Delicious, Ida Red, Jonagold, Jonathan, McIntosh and Rome.

Variation: Substitute 1 can (20 ounces) sliced Michigan Apples, drained and chopped for fresh Apples.

Favorite recipe from *Michigan Apple Committee*

Cheddar and Leek Strata

8 eggs, lightly beaten
2 cups milk
½ cup ale or beer
2 cloves garlic, minced
¼ teaspoon salt
¼ teaspoon black pepper
1 loaf (16 ounces) sourdough bread, cut into ½-inch cubes
2 small leeks, coarsely chopped
1 red bell pepper, chopped
1½ cups (6 ounces) shredded Swiss cheese
1½ cups (6 ounces) shredded sharp Cheddar cheese
Fresh sage sprigs for garnish

1. Combine eggs, milk, ale, garlic, salt and black pepper in large bowl. Beat until well blended.

2. Place ½ of bread cubes on bottom of greased 13×9-inch baking dish. Sprinkle ½ of leeks and ½ of bell pepper over bread cubes. Top with ¾ cup Swiss cheese and ¾ cup Cheddar cheese. Repeat layers with remaining ingredients, ending with Cheddar cheese.

3. Pour egg mixture evenly over top. Cover tightly with plastic wrap or foil. Weigh top of strata down with slightly smaller baking dish. Refrigerate strata at least 2 hours or overnight.

4. Preheat oven to 350°F. Bake, uncovered, 40 to 45 minutes or until center is set. Garnish with fresh sage, if desired. Serve immediately.

Makes 12 servings

The publisher would like to thank the companies and organizations listed below for the use of their recipes and photographs in this publication.

Almond Board of California
Barilla America, Inc.
BC-USA, Inc.
BelGioioso® Cheese, Inc.
Bob Evans®
California Asparagus Commission
California Table Grape Commission
California Tree Fruit Agreement
Chilean Fresh Fruit Association
Dole Food Company, Inc.
Duncan Hines® and Moist Deluxe® are registered trademarks of
Aurora Foods Inc.
Egg Beaters®
Florida's Citrus Growers
Guiltless Gourmet®
Hershey Foods Corporation
The Hidden Valley® Food Products Company
Hormel Foods, LLC
Keebler® Company
The Kingsford Products Company
Lawry's® Foods
McIlhenny Company (TABASCO® brand Pepper Sauce)
Michigan Apple Committee
Mushroom Information Center
National Honey Board
Norseland, Inc. / Lucini Italia Co.
Pear Bureau Northwest
Reckitt Benckiser Inc.
Reddi-wip® is a registered trademark of ConAgra Brands, Inc.
The J.M. Smucker Company
Property of © 2003 Sunkist Growers, Inc. All rights reserved.
Texas Peanut Producers Board
Uncle Ben's Inc.
Unilever Bestfoods North America

METRIC CONVERSION CHART

VOLUME MEASUREMENTS (dry)

$1/8$ teaspoon = 0.5 mL
$1/4$ teaspoon = 1 mL
$1/2$ teaspoon = 2 mL
$3/4$ teaspoon = 4 mL
1 teaspoon = 5 mL
1 tablespoon = 15 mL
2 tablespoons = 30 mL
$1/4$ cup = 60 mL
$1/3$ cup = 75 mL
$1/2$ cup = 125 mL
$2/3$ cup = 150 mL
$3/4$ cup = 175 mL
1 cup = 250 mL
2 cups = 1 pint = 500 mL
3 cups = 750 mL
4 cups = 1 quart = 1 L

VOLUME MEASUREMENTS (fluid)

1 fluid ounce (2 tablespoons) = 30 mL
4 fluid ounces ($1/2$ cup) = 125 mL
8 fluid ounces (1 cup) = 250 mL
12 fluid ounces ($1 1/2$ cups) = 375 mL
16 fluid ounces (2 cups) = 500 mL

WEIGHTS (mass)

$1/2$ ounce = 15 g
1 ounce = 30 g
3 ounces = 90 g
4 ounces = 120 g
8 ounces = 225 g
10 ounces = 285 g
12 ounces = 360 g
16 ounces = 1 pound = 450 g

DIMENSIONS

$1/16$ inch = 2 mm
$1/8$ inch = 3 mm
$1/4$ inch = 6 mm
$1/2$ inch = 1.5 cm
$3/4$ inch = 2 cm
1 inch = 2.5 cm

OVEN TEMPERATURES

250°F = 120°C
275°F = 140°C
300°F = 150°C
325°F = 160°C
350°F = 180°C
375°F = 190°C
400°F = 200°C
425°F = 220°C
450°F = 230°C

BAKING PAN SIZES

Utensil	Size in Inches/Quarts	Metric Volume	Size in Centimeters
Baking or Cake Pan (square or rectangular)	$8 \times 8 \times 2$	2 L	$20 \times 20 \times 5$
	$9 \times 9 \times 2$	2.5 L	$23 \times 23 \times 5$
	$12 \times 8 \times 2$	3 L	$30 \times 20 \times 5$
	$13 \times 9 \times 2$	3.5 L	$33 \times 23 \times 5$
Loaf Pan	$8 \times 4 \times 3$	1.5 L	$20 \times 10 \times 7$
	$9 \times 5 \times 3$	2 L	$23 \times 13 \times 7$
Round Layer Cake Pan	$8 \times 1 1/2$	1.2 L	20×4
	$9 \times 1 1/2$	1.5 L	23×4
Pie Plate	$8 \times 1 1/4$	750 mL	20×3
	$9 \times 1 1/4$	1 L	23×3
Baking Dish or Casserole	1 quart	1 L	—
	$1 1/2$ quart	1.5 L	—.
	2 quart	2 L	—

Metric chart